AF326548

<u>What They Said!</u>

"This book is a packet of dynamite. I've read a bunch on this subject, but nothing has hit me between the eyes like Randy Gage's Wealth Without Apology. If you're fighting your own self-limiting, programmed-from-childhood, unconscious compulsions (like I am), take two hours and immerse yourself in Mr. Gage's psychologically deep but proven-in-the-real-world principles and precepts. Randy is for real and so is his wisdom. Five stars!"

- Steven Pressfield
Bestselling author of *The War of Art*

"An absolutely must-read book for anyone ready for peak prosperity."

- Robin Sharma
#1 worldwide bestselling author of *The 5 AM Club and The Wealth Money Can't Buy*

"Wealth Without Apology explains why working hard to be our best selves is what prosperity is all about. Randy Gage provides this master class in living well across the spectrum—a terrific read at any stage of life and career."

- Harvey Mackay
Author of the New York Times #1 bestseller Swim with *The Sharks Without Being Eaten Alive*

"I can think of no one on the planet other than Randy Gage who understands the victimhood and poverty that lives between our ears and can move folks past it into an actionable plan that puts money in their pockets and brings financial freedom to their lives."

- Larry Winget
Six-time *NYT/WSJ* bestselling author & television personality

"I find myself saying this with every new book he releases, but...Randy Gage has done it again! This world-renowned prosperity mentor has taken his immense wisdom—honed through his own decades of embodying abundance after rising from its polar opposite—and turned it into a transformative, life-enhancing, and truly game-changing guide for living your best life. A proven methodology for cultivating greater happiness, vibrant health, and true wealth—in both mindset and material riches."

- Bob Burg
Coauthor of the international bestseller, *The Go-Giver, and author of Genuine Influence*

"There are critical forks in the road for all of us, and we sometimes are astute and lucky in our choice, and sometimes driven off the road altogether by outside pressures and internal doubts. Randy doesn't just help you take the right road, he provides you with the escape velocity to take off and soar.
He empowers you with purpose, power, and pragmatism."

- Alan Weiss, PhD
Author of *Million Dollar Consulting and fifty-four other books.*

"I always enjoy the books Randy Gage writes and I read them for new ideas, to confirm my thinking and/or challenge my thinking. Wealth Without Apology is no exception. It is a timely guide to gaining wealth and debunks so many of the bad ideas prosperity gurus espouse. It is a quick read that can change your thinking, and that can change everything."

- Mark Sanborn
International speaker and author of *The Fred Factor*

"I first learned about Randy's prosperity principles in 2007, when I thought they were crazy. I still think so, but now I know they're the crazy that wins championships and transforms businesses (mine being one of them). This book is a must-read for anyone looking to take a big leap to the next level in their lives."

- Jaime Lokier
Author of *Birthing Leaders*

"Reading Wealth Without Apology is like plugging into a power source and, guess what—that power source is you. I'm a believer in everything that's in this book, and it's wonderful to think of how many people's lives are going to change when they read it. One of Randy's mantras is 'Wake up wealthier each day than when you went to sleep the night before.' And you will become wealthier for having read this book."

- Joe Calloway
Author of Be the Best at *What Matters Most*

"Every so often you read a book that stops you in your tracks by speaking a truth you've been ignoring. Randy Gage's Wealth Without Apology did exactly that for me. It's a powerful, brave, wake-up call for anyone who's forgotten they're allowed to want more, dream bigger, and live without guilt. I'm grateful I got to experience it from the front row."

- Wes Linden
Acclaimed Entrepreneur, Executive Advisor and Host of *The Resilience Project podcast*

"Wow. I've got to tell you, this book hit me between the eyes. If you want a book on wealth that gently coaxes you into improvement, this is not it! In Randy's inimitable and distinctive style, he takes a two-by-four to your erroneous programming on money and prosperity. No matter where you are on life's pathway, Wealth Without Apology will create prosperity breakthroughs for you."

- Scott McKain

Speaker Hall of Fame, author of *Beyond Distinction and Iconic*
"Reading, thinking about, and remaining focused on one particular chapter each morning got me through one of my toughest, scariest, and most painful life experiences. This book helps fuel my passion and purpose in miraculous ways. Every day has become a masterclass in life!"

- Ann Feinstein
"The Leverage Queen"

"This book is about much more than money. It´s about your identity. It will teach you how to stop sabotaging the prosperity you deserve and will give you the tools to become the person truly capable of attracting it."

- Erick Gamio
Founder, REVOLVR

"He did it again! Wealth Without Apology shatters the limiting beliefs we inherit and exposes the excuses we cling to. Randy helped me break through barriers and achieve my wildest dreams in business and life. This book will do the same for you."

- Lisa Jimenez, M.Ed.
Founder, HOPE Publishing House, Luxury Retreat Facilitator

"More than a manifesto, make this your guidebook and action plan to prosperity, wealth, contribution, service, significance, and happiness. You should gift a copy of this book to everyone you love…at the earliest possible age!"

- Bill Bachrach
Hall of Fame keynote speaker & author of *Values-Based Financial Planning; The Art of Creating an Inspiring Financial Strategy*

"This book didn't just change my money mindset—it changed my life."

-Jeff Higginson
President, Rain International LLC

"Randy's life is his message. This book is intensely honest, wise, and direct. A true, practical map of how to create wealth and abundance in the 21st century. No motivation, no fluff, no woo-woo. Get ready for a deep conversation with yourself and be open to receive the abundance you deserve."

- Jose Lopez
Founder, Prosperity Global Team

"Twenty-five years ago, I found Randy Gage's first prosperity books. What a wakeup call in the best way. The world programs us for scarcity and victimhood, but Randy's work is the antidote. This book is a must read for anyone wanting total prosperity. And it is not a one-time read—this is a book I'll read every year.

- Dana Collins
Author, The Big Build

"As a songwriter, I am impressed with Randy's ability to communicate important ideas and his willingness to be vulnerable for the sake of those fortunate enough to read this book. His ideas are timeless and apply to everything we hope to achieve and become.

- Justin Rubenstein
BMG and Capital Records Recording Artist

Wealth Without Apology

A Prosperity Manifesto

Break the Programming
Reclaim Your Power
Live Rich on Purpose

New York Times Bestselling Author
Randy Gage

Copyright © 2026 by Randy Gage

All rights reserved.

Library of Congress Cataloging-in-Publication Data

Gage, Randy, author
Wealth Without Apology : A Prosperity Manifesto / Randy Gage. — First edition.
Miami, FL : Prosperity Factory Press, 2026.

ISBN 978-0-9979482-8-8

Self-help. 2. Personal growth. 3. Success. I. Title.

Published by Prosperity Factory Press
18117 Biscayne Blvd, Suite #4432
Miami, FL 33160
USA

First Edition

Printed in the United States of America

Table of Contents

<u>Dedication</u>

This book is dedicated to the person who knows there is a higher version of themselves waiting to be claimed. And who, once they rise into the health, happiness, and prosperity that is their birthright, will wear it proudly, without guilt, without fear, and without apology.

<u>Warning</u>

Reading this book could cause you to quit your job, hitchhike across a continent, run for president, divorce your spouse, change your career, come out of the closet, get a tattoo, renounce your religion, open a vinyl record store, end a relationship, start a movement, have a midlife crisis, become a tech billionaire, move to an ashram in India, adopt a child, or…all of the above.

Chapter 1:

The Only Free Cheese Is In The Mousetrap

At fifteen years old, I was languishing in a jail cell, waiting on a trial date for multiple charges, including burglary and armed robbery. The depressing cell had a metal door containing a small window near the top with safety glass and wires. Through that window I would sit on my cot, watching the tick, tick, tick of the second hand, as it circled around a clock in the hallway outside. As you might imagine, this situation created ideal timing, at a very young age, to rethink the trajectory of my life.

There's a very good chance you picked up this book because this is the perfect time to rethink the trajectory of your own life. (Whether you're fifteen, or fifty-five, or a hundred and five.)

At fifteen, I was already a profuse user of drugs and alcohol who had made some ill-fated choices. But more germane to this discussion, I was an angry adolescent, furious at a society that didn't offer equality for all. (Meaning me, of course.) I went to school with kids whose parents bought them go-karts and motorcycles, had their own bedrooms, and went on vacations to cool places. My mom, raising three kids by herself, could never offer a lifestyle like that.

No one even knew what autism was back then, but I was on the spectrum, blessed with both a genius IQ and a complete inability to understand, interact, and relate with the species known as human. Even at an early age, it was obvious that I was smarter than my teachers and counselors, so I discounted their attempts to help me, choosing instead to look for shortcuts, ways to jump the line, and somehow catch up to those who had a higher standard of living. Pulling a weapon on a cashier and walking out with $800 in sixty seconds seemed like a much more effective way to equalize the economic opportunity than those hard, boring, and slow ways everyone else was doing. And that worked great.

Until it didn't.

That experience blessed me in countless ways, but perhaps the most important was the life philosophy that came out of it. Understanding that while there is tremendous inequality in this world, you don't have to be powerless to it. There are actions you can take to level the playing field. There is a value-for-value exchange aspect to the Universe, and once you understand that, you can achieve all the manifestations of true prosperity.

Which is my hope for you when you read this book…

Maybe you're arriving at this moment angry and disillusioned, maybe you don't think life is fair, maybe you're wondering what the hell you have to do to catch a break. That's okay. But understand this…

There are no government programs, medical procedures, or postgraduate courses to treat you for prosperity—you must be open to receiving it.

I'll do my best to help you make that mental transformation. This is not a money, finance, or investment book. Nor am I accredited, certified, or licensed as anything. I'm a high school dropout who went from broke to balling, and this is a book about prosperity. It's written to get up in your grill, to change the way you think—not just about money but the entire spectrum of abundant living. And more importantly, to help you stop judging yourself or feeling guilty for wanting to create a better life for you and your loved ones.

Fair warning…

You should know that this process will eventually lead you to a fork in the road offering two choices: victimhood or victory.

Victimhood offers many benefits. More people will relate to you, you'll get to commiserate in victim marathons with others, and the people on social media will adore you. However, at some point you'll come to terms with the reality that the only free cheese is in the mousetrap. Being a professional victim can give you a sense of identity, even provide you with a perverse sense of virtue, because you're always the lone hero, fighting the forces of evil.

But as tantalizing as these benefits might appear through that distorted thinking, you must reject them entirely to become a victor.

The benefits of being a victor are simple yet quite profound: You will live a healthy, happy, and prosperous life.

What I'm about to tell you may seem counterintuitive, shocking, or unbelievable, but I promise you with every fiber of my being it is true:

The single most important variable for living a prosperous life is not where you were born, the wealth of your family, your connections, or your education level. It is your mindset.

While the statistics about inequality for women, minorities, etc., may be true, they only measure what happened…not what could have happened—especially for an individual within any discriminated-against group. Any person in one of those groups can choose to be successful despite the odds. And many do, because they adjust their mindset. They recognize that agency—the ability to make decisions and act independently in an oppressively controlled system designed to keep someone in servitude—can be the breakthrough to a prosperous life. They understand that powerful, seemingly omnipotent forces like the government, monetary system, and a controlling society cannot prevent them from becoming healthy, happy, and prosperous if they are so determined.

As you can imagine, this requires a dramatic mental readjustment…

A big element in this readjustment is sharpening your ability to learn how to think. For your entire life, governments, the education system, banking system, media ecosystem, even the people who care about you…have been trying to teach you what to think, not how to think. You cannot allow yourself to be provoked or directed by the random thoughts bombarding you daily. You must become mindful enough to think about what you think about.

Ultimately, to manifest an abundant life, you must become "the thinker of the thought."

You are now using your mind instead of being used by your mind—because you can pause, rise above your thoughts, and be conscious of them. Psychologists have known for decades that people with an internal locus of control—the belief that they influence their outcomes—outperform, out-earn, and outlive those who believe life just "happens" to them. Your mindset rewires your destiny. This is why the stats for a particular group may suck…but some people in that group succeed anyway. You are not a statistic…or a victim of the stats. You are you, a category of one.

Healthy people think differently than sick people.
Happy people think differently than depressed people.
Wealthy people think differently than broke people.

You might think your body and circumstances control your thoughts, but it's the opposite.

Enlightened, prosperous, self-actualized people create their lives by the power of thought. For most of us, by the time we have reached our teenage years, we've become conditioned into being victims of circumstance.

When you become the thinker of the thought, you become the architect of your life. You stop believing in fate, luck, and happenstance and start realizing that you're a co-creator of your life. Agency defeats victimhood.

And that's where the transformation happens.

The world needs you to be healthy.
The world needs you to be happy.
The world needs you to be rich.

You up for that?

Chapter 2:

Poverty Sucks. (Stop Making It a Lifestyle Choice.)

If you're ready to reject the free cheese and create a prosperous life for yourself, it's necessary to first kill some poverty myths and moral poisoning about money and success. Let's start with the nonsensical idea that poverty is intrinsically saintly.

It's not.

Poverty causes people to lie, cheat, steal, and even kill. Contrary to the romantic myths, there is nothing inherently noble, virtuous, or spiritual about poverty.

You're frequently exposed to tropes like "money doesn't buy happiness." That's true, but please don't take that to mean that somehow poverty buys happiness, because that's delusional bullshit.

While happiness doesn't come from money and material things, the freedom and self-expression they offer you can make you decidedly happier.

I know what it's like to live in poverty and what it's like to live a life of prosperity. Anyone who doesn't recognize that prosperity is better has been brainwashed to a level of ignorance that is dangerous to themselves and the rest of us as well. In fact, the world would be a much better place if everyone woke up each morning and screamed "FUCK POVERTY!!!" out loud ten times. (And as my friend Bill Bachrach pointed out after reading an early draft of this book, middle class sucks too. Why would anyone make a conscious decision to be average, middle, or mediocre when greatness is possible? Ain't nothing noble about that. So… FUCK THE MIDDLE TOO!!!)

If you are starting to feel that I'm coming in too hot, too fast, please know that it's not because I'm here to insult you or demean your situation. As you read further, you'll discover that almost no one possessed more toxic beliefs, or made more foolish mistakes along the journey than I did. I'm writing this book because I genuinely want the world we share to be a more prosperous place. And I don't think that happens with pandering, participation trophies, or entitlement programs. We make the world more prosperous when we help the people of the world live more prosperously. That means real transformation, and while transformation happens through education and enlightenment, it begins with truth. No progress happens without the stone-cold truth.

Please allow me to perhaps challenge some of your most sacred, emotional, deeply held beliefs. Because those beliefs are the ones that determine whether you live in lack or abundance.

I fervently believe that abundant prosperity is the birthright and natural state of every creature on Earth. And I also believe the reason most people (perhaps including you) don't accept this birthright is because they have countless levels of subconscious programming and are still clinging to the false premise that being poor is noble, virtuous, and/or even spiritual. We'll explore this issue deeper in the chapters ahead, but it's important that you know my fundamental posit about negative programming.

When people read my earlier book, Radical Rebirth, they're shellshocked to learn the suffocating amount of this insidious programming that they're exposed to on a minute-by-minute basis. Media researchers have found that wealthy characters in movies and TV are portrayed as villains about four times more often than heroes—and kids absorb that long before they ever make their first dollar. (Much more about this later too.) You are receiving this prejudiced programming constantly from the government, education system, organized religion, and what I'll call the datasphere: blogs, books, podcasts, TV shows, movies, and both traditional and social media.

Between the ages of two and eight, you're bombarded with literally thousands (possibly millions) of subliminal messages denigrating money and wealthy people and exalting poverty and poor people. As a result, you probably developed your core foundational beliefs about the most important things in life—love, health, happiness, relationships, etc.—before you blew out the candles on your ninth birthday.

As a child, were you told things like "money doesn't grow on trees" or your family didn't qualify for nice things? You probably were jealous or hateful of rich people before you got your first allowance.

Was there physical or mental abuse or cheating behavior between your parents? Your core beliefs about marriage and relationships were likely set before you were ever in a relationship yourself.

Were sex and nudity taboo subjects in your home growing up? You were probably a mess of sexual hang-ups before you reached puberty.

Did you attend some type of youth religious programing that taught you were born a sorry sinner? Or not worthy of God's love unless you spent your whole lifetime prostrating for forgiveness so you could get rewarded in the afterlife? What did that do for your self-esteem before you even reached your teen years?

Reverend Charles Fillmore shocked the religious community of his day when he stated it is a sin to be poor. Seminar audiences of today are still offended when I reaffirm this. But if we explore the true definition of sin, you might change your mind on the subject.

Everyone seems to believe that the Bible was written in whatever their first language is, but the primary content was composed in Aramaic. The Aramaic way sin is written in the Bible is best translated as "missing the mark." For my metaphysical friends, A Course in Miracles defines sin as "a lack of love." I believe both definitions are appropriate, because when you're poor, you truly are missing the mark—missing out on the love offered by the force that created you.

Most of the world is behaving as if the opposite were true. This behavior is fueled by erroneous beliefs:

- They believe that depriving themselves of money and material goods is required to receive the blessing of their God.

- Or they may believe that they are meant to suffer during their lifetimes in the physical realm to be prosperous in some spiritual realm, such as an afterlife or reincarnation.

- They might have a subconscious fear that, should they become wealthy, it would cause their loved ones to stop loving them.

- They believe money and prosperity are finite.

- Some suffer from a guilt complex, thinking that out-earning their parents would dishonor them.

- They've been subconsciously programmed to believe money or rich people are inherently evil.

- Many others have experienced physical or emotional abuse in their formative years and their self-esteem has been so shattered that they believe they are not worthy or deserving of a happy prosperous life.

- Sometimes they develop worthiness issues from the guilt trips used against them when they are successful.

- They believe that for abundance to come to them, it must be at the expense of someone else.

These are all batshit-crazy level beliefs and if you unknowingly possess them, you will almost certainly self-sabotage your success and happiness without ever knowing you are doing it.

As if these limiting beliefs weren't enough, there is also a strong probability you have encountered another tripwire...
*Most of the world has adopted one of two overall premises

about the role of money in prosperity. Surprisingly, although they conflict with each other, neither one is right. They are both bad premises, even though about 80 percent of the world believes one or the other.

The first bad premise is that money isn't required for prosperity. This is false. The second bad premise is that if you amass enough money, you can buy your way to happiness. Also false.

Allowing yourself to be influenced by either of these erroneous premises is destructive to your health, happiness, and prosperity.

Let's double-click on them...

The meme that money isn't required for prosperity is damaging because it causes you to climb the wrong mountain. Any plan built on the belief that money is not necessary for a prosperous life is destined for failure. Yet this theory is still frequently disseminated by many authors, seminar leaders, and spiritual gurus. They make inane statements like, "We were poor but there was so much love in our home we didn't know it," "I may not have any money, but I have my health and great relationships," or, "Money doesn't buy happiness."

They probably mean well, but their ignorance is harmful to themselves and those who follow them. Their premise that money isn't integral to prosperity is basically a recipe for a limiting vision and is a gateway drug to a life of self-sabotage. (Where you are subsisting on the emotional payoff of living in victimhood.)

Let's be very, very clear…

If you don't know where you're going to find the rent money, can't afford proper medical care, or your kids can't play safely in your neighborhood—you're not even in the postal code of the abundant life that should be your birthright.

Now let's explore bad premise number two, the idea that money will solve all your problems. Not. A. Chance.

Money can solve your money problems. (But only once you've learned how the money game is played.) Money won't solve your addiction problems, toxic relationships, or worthiness issues. And a convincing case can be made that money will likely make these situations worse. (Not that I would know anything about that!

Although if we explore yet deeper, it should be noted that money actually can help even with things like addiction or relationship issues—because it can allow you to receive good-quality care from the right professionals.

If you subscribe to either of these beliefs above, you are insulating yourself from the mindset you are going to need for a breakthrough—because true prosperity is holistic, an intoxicating mélange of four major quadrants of living, one of which is money and material things. (Which we'll explore in a later chapter.)

Unfortunately, there is so much programming to shame you regarding money, success, and even happiness, it's easy to fall into self-sabotage behavior. Please understand this…
You were born to live a rich life. That includes having

basic security, sleeping well, eating nourishing foods, living in a harmonious environment, wearing appropriate clothing, enjoying optimal health, and nurturing positive relationships.

- Your need to feel secure is valid. This is a human right everyone deserves.

- Your quest to be recognized for achievement does not mean you're narcissistic. It is healthy.

- Your yearning to be energetic, mentally sharp, and fit is a birthright. Don't be self-conscious about it.

- Your desire to be happy is natural. There is no need to explain, justify, or defend this to anyone.

Don't let anyone or anything guilt, shame, or ridicule you for seeking these things. Anyone or anything that attempts to do so is toxic and dangerous to you and should be removed from your circle of influence immediately.

To manifest an abundant life, you must blow up limiting beliefs that romanticize poverty, struggle, or victimhood—and replace them with empowering beliefs that respect the benefits of becoming healthy, happy, and rich.

I'll posit that true happiness is created by self-fulfillment within yourself. More specifically, you need to have a tangible vision for the good you will create by living and modeling a prosperous life and how you can use that abundance to become the highest possible version of yourself.

Because becoming the highest possible version of yourself is how you best contribute to the world.

Every day you wake up, the Universe is greeting you with a very simple yet profound question...

"How much prosperity are you willing to accept today?"

When people are presented this all-you-can-eat prosperity buffet, it's shocking how many just nibble a few bites. Why? Because of all those limiting beliefs in the list above (and others). They view the world through such a small window that they can't drink in the greatness that's out there for them. I can testify to this from personal experience...

In 1959, two cataclysmic events occurred that forever changed the course of human history. Okay, maybe not all human history, but at least my human history.

On April 6th of that year, I entered the world. Then on October 15th, Simon & Schuster published The Magic of Thinking BIG, by David J. Schwartz. Two seemingly unrelated occurrences, but a few decades later, they would intersect to rock my world...

You may have been in the audience for one of my keynotes and heard me tell the story of how I made $250,000 in twenty minutes. Or perhaps you've heard one of my Prosperity TV podcast episodes sharing the experience of flying on the Concorde to London for a weekend of shoe shopping. (Fortunately, if you haven't, that story is coming soon...to a chapter near you!) Or just maybe you read my blog about gifting a $60k watch to someone at one of my seminars.

You should know that the only reason all three of those

scenarios came about is because I read that book by Dr. Schwartz.

Truth is, when I read the book again recently, it landed as a little simplistic, even corny. But at the consciousness level I was operating with when I first read it—that modest book was the equivalent of cognitive ontology, molecular biology, and quantum physics to me.

It wasn't because the book broke down any scientific processes about wealth building, provided guidance on how to navigate the entrepreneurial world, or outlined the roadmap to success. The book simply does what the title promises: teaches you that there is a tangible benefit in thinking BIG. Giving yourself permission to dream again. And to dream bigger.

Please. Allow this book to do for you what the Schwartz book did for me.

You can recognize the limiting beliefs you hold, blow them up, and send them back to the nothingness from which they came. Replace them with beliefs that empower you. You can recognize the self-sabotage pattern you've been on and halt it immediately. Society takes its cues from you. People will respect, value, and appreciate you to the same degree you respect, value, and appreciate yourself.

The day you understand this insight is the day that transforms your life forever.

Before we move into the following chapters, please allow me to share one of the most profound lessons on prosperity you will ever learn…

It is easier to earn a large amount of money quickly than it is to earn a small amount of money slowly.

Really.

It's easier to sell a $3 million Bugatti than a Kia for $25,000. It's easier to market a $40,000 speech than a $5,000 one. It's easier to sell an $8 million home than a $250,000 one. If you have any doubts, speak to someone with domain expertise in these areas and they'll confirm this is true.

Really.

When I began my speaking career, I used to sell seminars for $27. You'd be amazed how many people wouldn't register without doing a thirty-minute phone consultation (interrogation) with me. Now I sell seminars for $25,000 and people register online without even speaking to a human.

When I charged $5,000 a month for consulting, we had to hunt down the payments almost every month. When I went up to $40-50k a month, we attracted clients who always send payment before it's due.

When I did a $1,500 coaching program, not only did we have to chase down people to get paid, but also for them to do the homework and participate. When we went to $25k, compliance went up. When we broke the $100k price, the issues evaporated. You'll discover the reasons for this in the chapter on magnitude of scale.

But first, allow me to interject something important...

One of the early readers of the galley proof for this book responded with a concern that you might read this section, jack up your fees, and price yourself out of the market. And that could happen if you're not solving real problems or providing true value. But the much more frequent scenario is people who are solving real problems and providing real value are simply being timid and incremental about how and how much they ask to be compensated.

He suggested that you would need to be selling speeches for $5k before you could offer them for $40k. While that is the case 90 percent of the time, it doesn't have to be so. Early in my career, I was crisscrossing the country, flying economy, doing all-day seminars for $37. Then I attended a Jay Abraham Boot Camp for $25k. (Which I had to split with someone and still put most of the cost on a credit card.) I came home afterward and immediately started promoting my own $15k Boot Camp for high-level achievers in the network marketing profession. No one in that space had ever charged more than $100 for a program. Ever. Friends were calling me, suggesting I had lost my mind.

Until the program sold out.

My friend's premise: Prosperity cannot deny a process. My response: True, but the process is in YOU, not anything external.

There are millions of examples to support my thesis, but most you've never heard of, because they're people not doing anything to showboat their success, just going about their business, doing their thing. They're bold, ballsy, and impatient. They aren't willing to take the conventional, incremental process, because they have high self-esteem and know the value of their work.

By the way, taking bold actions can be scary. Because sometimes you must create a vacuum for the Universe to fill it with good. You might suffer some short-term loss when you first step up to your new levels of worth. But if you're not willing to lose your $1k clients, you'll never attract the $10k ones. (We'll do a deeper dive on this in Chapter Seven.)

- You weren't born to play small.
- You weren't created to struggle.
- You were meant to be prosperous.

Know your worth. Then add the VAT tax.

And when you finally do, you'll realize the shocking truth:

Prosperity isn't just a goal—it's your spiritual obligation.

Chapter 3:

Why Living Rich Is a Spiritual Quest

When you think of spirituality, does the concept conjure up words such as bliss, enlightenment, nirvana, or harmony? I hope so, because living a rich life should be viewed with that type of perspective.

Many people believe that to build a more prosperous world, we should all seek less, consume less, and stop being so selfish. What if I told you that this belief is holding back humanity and is actually incredibly selfish and detrimental to the world and greater good?

I believe that living rich is not just your right, but your sacred responsibility.

As I mentioned in Chapter One, the world needs you, and me, and as many other people as possible to live rich. This is one of the first principles of the Universe. In fact, not unfolding into your potential is a crime against the very nature of the

Universe. This was eloquently expressed back in 1910 by Wallace D. Wattles in his book, The Science of Getting Rich, when he said:

"Every living thing must continually seek for the enlargement of its life, because life, in the mere act of living, must increase itself.

"A seed, dropped on the ground, springs into activity, and in the act of living produces a hundred more seeds; life, by living, multiplies itself. It is forever Becoming More; it must do so, if it continues to be at all.

"Intelligence is under this same necessity for continuous increase. Every thought we think makes it necessary for us to think another thought; consciousness is continually expanding. Every fact we learn leads us to the learning of another fact; knowledge is continually increasing. Every talent we cultivate brings to the mind the desire to cultivate another talent; we are subject to the urge of life, seeking expression, which ever drives us on to know more, to do more, and to be more.

"In order to know more, do more, and be more, we must have more; we must have things to use, for we learn, and do, and become, only by using things. We must get rich, so that we can live more."

In all living organisms, stasis eventually equals death. To make the world more prosperous requires each of us continually seeking to manifest our own prosperity. We're not going to save the planet by renouncing electricity and moving back into thatched huts. We'll save the planet by becoming more prosperous through growth, innovation, and progress. I'll go yet further and argue that if you or I are not growing and expanding, we're a drag on everyone else, making their lives (and world progress) more difficult.

Speaking of progress, Gandhi once said healthy discontent is the prelude to creating it. This holds true for manifesting prosperity. Unfolding into your greatest good involves a concept called Divine Discontent. Divine Discontent is the state of mind in which you can live in gratitude for what you have yet still have an innate hunger and desire to do, have, and become more, as Wattles referenced.

This yearning for more causes you to develop bigger dreams. Those bigger dreams require you to grow more to achieve them. You find your thinking to that point won't get you to where you want to go. This causes you to develop new thought processes and create a perpetual cycle of improvement— which is where the breakthroughs live.

Going through this process toward prosperity can be an inspiring spiritual experience, because it's as if you're communing with the force that created you. It doesn't really matter what label you assign that force. Call it God, Nature, the Universe, or whatever aligns with your core beliefs. I posit that it is the desire of this force that you become prosperous, because only when you reach the higher levels of prosperity can that force be best expressed in you. The more mental harmony, resources, money, and optimal health you possess, the more you can provide expression of that force.

And I'd argue further that remaining poor (or sick or unhappy) is an insult to that same force.

Think of your life as a spiritual pursuit, one in which you face an ongoing series of challenges and tests. These trials help to chisel away your base elements to reveal and polish your higher elements—that which is true, virtuous, and enlightened about you. I believe a natural result of a journey such as this should be an abundance of money and material things.

This is not to suggest that it is inherently noble to be rich. That premise is as irrational as believing it is inherently noble to be poor. What I am suggesting is that true prosperity means evolving into the highest possible version of yourself—and seeking wealth is a noble and necessary element in that journey. Because money and material things give you freedom to express yourself, they also give you the opportunity to live your most spiritual life. (Speaking only about spirituality here, not religion.)

Most people understand that being rich offers better choices and freedom from the tyranny of debt. Unfortunately, the aspect of wealth that remains hidden to them is its capacity to accelerate your personal growth and development. Setting an intention to become wealthy is a noble pursuit that can lead to greater spiritual fulfillment. It also allows you to expand the prosperity of the entire world. Solving problems…especially the biggest problems in the world…requires money and influence to tackle. If you really care about peace, hunger, climate change, etc., the more successful you are personally, the more likely you can make an impact on improving these issues for us all.

If everyone in the world got a massage every week, there would be no war…

If everyone had time for quiet meditation or prayer each day, imagine how much more empathy and understanding there would be in the world...

If every child received access to safe water and adequate nutrition,think of the amazing contributions they could bring to our world...

Money and material things eliminate a lot of unnecessary stress and anxiety, allowing you to nurture the spiritual elements of your life. We recognize the need to pay plumbers, doctors, and bus drivers for the role they play in our lives. Why can't we do a better job rewarding dancers, sculptors, and poets for the contributions they make to our greater good? I celebrate the free enterprise system and believe it's the best framework to operate a village, nation, or world. Yet I often wonder if there's a way to incorporate a universal basic income that would allow more artists to contribute to society in a better way. (Without falling prey to the free cheese dynamic. Actually on second thought, let's just get more of them to read this book!)

Earlier we made a distinction between spirituality and religion, but I believe prosperity can enhance religion in many tangible ways. Think of all the limiting money beliefs found in religion.

What kind of underlying mindset must be in place to cause expressions like poor as a church mouse to become clichés? Why do so many believe that people who run charities and religious institutions should subsist on lower salaries? If you're pulling into the parking lot of a house of worship for a sermon, you should be hoping that the person giving it is driving the Lambo, not the rusted-out broke-mobile parked next to it. And if you're starting a nonprofit organization to end hunger, save the rainforests, or provide medical services to indigent children—wouldn't you want to offer a salary competitive enough to attract the best and brightest people on Earth to run it?

The meek won't inherit the earth if they're making the minimum payments on their credit card balances each month. Or choosing between enough medicine or food.

Poverty is evil. Prosperity is spirituality in action.

Playing small and living in poverty isn't humility. (In fact, it's false humility.) True humility is about loving your neighbor and seeking the greater good, which means striving to become the highest possible version of yourself. That highest possible version of yourself will never be complete until you are manifesting a prosperous life. And psychologically, humility isn't about demeaning yourself but rather seeing the worth in others.

Your desire to do, have, and become more is a wake-up call from the force that created you. An invitation to step into your spiritual calling. And that's why living a prosperous life is your spiritual quest.

In my case, before I could understand prosperity as a spiritual calling, I had to meet its opposite face to face. And that's how I ended up in a crack house in Liberty City…

Chapter 4:

You Didn't Get Here by Accident: How Micro-Decisions Shape Your Destiny

Once an urban myth takes hold, it never seems to die—for instance, the one that says an undercover agent must admit that they're a police officer if you ask them outright. (I guess the people who believe this have never seen an episode of The Wire or Miami Vice.) So, it was no surprise that as I negotiated a deal with a drug dealer for the sixth time, he asked me—for the sixth time—if I was an undercover police officer. After assuring him I wasn't, he produced an eight-ball of crystal meth, which I replaced with cash.

Just a hunch, but this probably isn't the type of story you were expecting to read in a prosperity book. But there's a powerful lesson here...

Because...I wasn't mystically transported into that crack house in Liberty City by fate, accident, or random happenstance. As

James Clear demonstrated with his book, Atomic Habits, tiny daily choices compound into wildly different futures—which is exactly what landed me in such a desperate and dangerous place that night. You could even argue that this was the logical result of hundreds of seemingly inconsequential small daily decisions I had made along the way.

Which leads us to the bad news and the good news...

The bad news is that, like me, the state of your prosperity or lack of it in your life right now is no accident. The good news is that, like me, the state of your prosperity or lack of it in your life right now is no accident. We are both irrefutable proof of what James Allen asserted decades ago: *Your life is created by the thoughts you give precedence to.*

Using the power of thought is the path to manifesting true prosperity in your life. Because you can't attain health, happiness, and wealth without directing the everyday thoughts that allow you to create them—or repel them.

It's astonishing how few people recognize the foundational limiting beliefs they possess. And going deeper, the thoughts that they then give precedence to. Allen used the garden analogy: If you allow your garden to develop on its own, it will likely get overgrown with weeds. But if you cultivate it, you can grow prosperity-inducing fruits, vegetables, or flowers.

People often complain about the circumstances they are fighting. Unfortunately, they're frequently fighting the effect but nourishing and preserving the cause. That cause could be an unconscious belief like thinking you are not worthy, money is bad, or that it is spiritual to be poor. (You should know I am the world's preeminent expert on this topic, because I lived in my own state of denial for more than thirty-five years.)

Unless and until you deal with the cause, the effect is going to keep coming back.

Doing sketchy deals in crack houses was simply the result of my losing sight of who I could become and falling prey to negative, self-destructive beliefs instead. (Which led to self-destructive decisions, which led to self-destructive habits, which led to self-destructive results.) Those beliefs would have eventually killed me, so I was forced to reexamine them.

There are always external factors you can blame for the bad shit going on in your life. If you're not manifesting the level of prosperity you desire, it's easy to dump the blame on the economy, your ex-spouse, bad luck, the curse of Macbeth, or some other external factor.

But if we're being honest, we both know that you didn't get here by accident…

We live in a time of fluctuating economies, erratic stock markets, and government deficits. That's because all times are like that. We'll never be at a loss of tsunamis, tornadoes, earthquakes, hurricanes, and erupting volcanoes either. And there will always be jealous friends who begrudge your success, petty people who may subconsciously want to sabotage you, even evil souls who wish to harm you. (Hell, if you haven't attracted some haters by now, you must be living a pretty timid life.)

Those are all great excuses for not being successful, but

they're still excuses. Everyone in life faces challenges like these, but not everyone elects to overcome them.

Yes, there will sometimes be random events that you have no control over, like a sinkhole swallowing your house or a meteorite landing on your new Toyota. Overall, though, the number of things that happen in our lives we don't attract, create, or have a strong influence on is shockingly minuscule.

While there sometimes are random events, there are no random lives.

Many people get defensive about this truth and look for chance exceptions—like those mentioned above—to argue against the point. This is an extremely harmful life strategy, because there are outliers to almost every situation. More importantly, if you're making this argument, it means you're refusing to accept responsibility for your life.

To manifest prosperity, we must accept that we truly are the co-creators of our lives, contributing in large part to both the things we say we don't want and those we do. And once you do that, it's a lot easier to increase the positive part of the equation. This frees you up to learn how to cope with emotions, take care of your health and mindset, and develop healthier relationships as well as a higher self-awareness. These are all areas you can influence greatly, and they are the life skills that best help you navigate your way to a prosperous life.

One of the negative aspects of ego is our acute fear of change. We'll desperately cling to the status quo, even when it's no longer working. Sometimes even when it never worked.

Don't live in denial by thinking your life is a random happenstance or that you have a positive vision and expectations but are constantly experiencing negative outcomes by some exception to universal laws. Tragedies, accidents, and misfortunes can happen to anyone, but endless cycles of those events occur only to people who co-create them with their negative expectations and/or because they're getting some kind of emotional payoff.

Ideally, we should be continually reinventing ourselves through life as we evolve through mental and emotional growth. This should result in an advancing career, more fulfilling relationships, higher earnings, greater self-awareness, and, ultimately, a more harmonious life.
But if you think you're reinventing yourself yet still end up creating the same results, it means you have subconscious programming that is distorting your thinking and causing you to self-sabotage.

If you want to grow into the highest possible version of yourself, you must get out of denial and recognize the contribution you are making to both the good and bad events happening in your life. Once you accept this premise above, it's a lot easier to increase the positive part of the equation. Begin with the premise of this chapter:

You didn't get here by accident. Your current situation in life—rich or poor, healthy or sick, happy or depressed— is the direct result of the micro-decisions you've made along the way.

The most influential element of the decisions you make is your vision. This vision, which you now know was probably developed as a young child, determines whether you exercise or don't, eat celery or Krispy Kreme, have healthy or dysfunctional relationships, and vacation at the Ritz Carlton or the Motel 6. Unfortunately, sometimes it's not a clear trajectory that's immediately predictable. It's a zigzag, tumultuous journey, created incrementally by millions of seemingly inconsequential experiences, actions, and micro-decisions.

Everyone has a vision for their life, even those who believe they don't. What many don't understand is that a vision isn't always an optimistic visualization of an idealized future. That's only one possible type; there are two others: neutral and negative.

A surprisingly large number of people in the world hold a neutral vision. They usually argue that they don't have a vision, but that's because they don't recognize they're holding a neutral one. (It's hard to read the label when you're inside the bottle.) They expect little from life, and that's what they manifest. If they have goals, they're small, pedestrian ones. Their driving motivation might be getting through the week without getting fired, so they can binge on Netflix all weekend without thinking of their lives of quiet desperation until the alarm goes off Monday morning. For them, life is just something that happens to them.

A troubling number of people have a negative vision. They expect bad things to happen in their life, so of course they do. They subscribe to the philosophy life's a bitch and then you die.

People with a negative vision revel in victimhood and never miss an opportunity to regale you with stories of their latest layoff, medical condition, or horrific traffic accident. Their vision becomes a self-fulfilling prophecy, reinforcing their negative beliefs.

The people in the neutral and negative vision groups consciously or subconsciously create a negative or neutral worldview that shapes the rest of their lives. If they don't get a strong enough jolt to question their beliefs, they follow a path spiraling downward into illness, poverty, and misery.

Much as the negative-vision people create a self-fulfilling prophecy of doom, the people with a positive vision create a self-fulfilling prophecy of prosperity. They expect good things to happen in their lives, and for the most part they do.

The fact you're still reading this book at this point suggests that you're now ready to create a new and more empowering vision. To do that, you must begin with your core foundational beliefs—how you got them and are still getting them.

You didn't just snap your fingers and build an instant vision for yourself. Whether that vision is positive, negative, or neutral, you've developed it over the course of your life, beginning as a young child.

First, recognize you are being programmed (brainwashed) 24/7, and this programming causes you to develop core foundational beliefs. Second, these core foundational beliefs help you form your perspective of the world. (Your vision.) Next, your vision determines the daily habits you adopt. Finally, your daily habits create your destiny. (Which you've subconsciously created to match your vision.) It becomes a self-fulfilling prophecy.

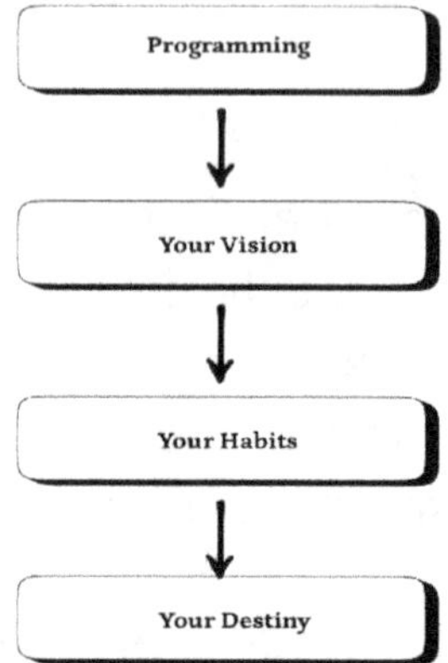

To change your life, you must change your vision. And to do that, you must reverse-engineer the process going back to the core foundational beliefs you were programmed with, probably as a child, and never questioned since. (Unless you had a cataclysmic failure to shock you into self-introspection.) For most people, that programming came from five major sources:

1. Your family of origin, friends, coaches, etc.
2. Government
3. The education system
4. Organized religion
5. The datasphere (social media, movies, television podcasts, blogs, etc.)

Source one, the original, is usually the most potent and effective builder of your overall perspective on (and vision for) your life. As we discussed earlier, your core, foundational beliefs about all the important elements of life were all mostly developed and cemented before you turned eight.

It may seem far-fetched to think that life-altering events in your thirties or forties, such as divorce, bankruptcy, or Type 2 diabetes, could simply be the logical result of beliefs you developed when you were six or seven. But that's probably reality. (After interacting with millions of people through my speeches, books, podcasts, and blogs, I'd wager that beliefs created in childhood and never reexamined are the cause of adult dysfunction a huge amount of the time).

At first glance, most people doubt the level of programming they have received because all those five sources above are supposed to help protect and care for them. That's true superficially. But unfortunately, the people who make up those categories (friends, family, teachers, preachers, coaches, etc.) are, unbeknownst to them, also programmed with thousands of negative, limiting beliefs. Most of these influencers are simply disseminating the visions they developed from their own source one.

When we break down sources two through five, we discover that these institutions and entities are often run by other brainwashed humans who are repeating the negative cycle of their own programming origins. (And you already know what the effects of this are from Chapter Two.)

So where do you receive positive, empowering, prosperous programming?

If you're like most people, almost nowhere. Let this book be a start. Then you're going to need to seek out many more sources of input that speak to health, happiness, and prosperity. Look for blogs, podcasts, biographies of those who lived lives you'd like to emulate, and surround yourself with people who call you to the higher side of you, not the base elements.

For you to receive the most powerful breakthroughs possible, start by analyzing your core foundational beliefs in six categories. The beliefs you hold in these six categories do about 90 percent of the heavy lifting in terms of carving out the window you view the world through. (I teased this info in Chapter Two. Let's bring it into better focus.)

In no particular order, they are:

1. Money and Success

2. Work and Career

3. Sex and Sexuality

4. Health and Wellness

5. God and Religion

6. Marriage and Relationships

Did your parents affirm things like "money doesn't grow on trees" and "we can't afford that?" You probably had feelings of jealousy (or even hate) for wealthy people before you were six and are likely living in poverty consciousness today. And, if by chance, you start to become wealthy, you'll subconsciously sabotage yourself to prevent becoming one of those evil, mean, rich people you despise.

Were you led to believe that to build a successful career requires you to be a terrible parent? Or that profitable companies must exploit workers, evade taxes, and plunder the environment? Imagine what those core beliefs will do if you try any entrepreneurial endeavor.

Was sex a taboo subject in your home growing up? Were you taught conventional roles like boys play with trucks and become doctors and girls play with dolls and become nurses? You were a mess of hang-ups, gender bias, and dysfunctional sexual beliefs before you even knew what orgasm meant.

When you were a child, was 90 percent of the food in your pantry manufactured substances like breakfast cereals, toaster pastries, and dry goods with an expiration date three years in the future? Did the role models in your life carry an extra five pounds for every decade older they were? Did your grandparents (or even parents) have ten (or more!) different prescriptions they took daily? If so, you're probably already well on your way to obesity, heart disease, and diabetes—because of your core foundational beliefs.

Were you raised in a religious household and taught concepts that essentially led you to believe you are not worthy? You're likely dealing with low self-esteem and self-sabotaging every serious attempt you make toward happiness.

Did you grow up in a single-parent household, experience your parents divorcing, or know that one of them was cheating on the other? You crystallized core beliefs about marriage and romantic relationships before you ever experienced your first one. And you're likely already repeating the dysfunction.

To live an abundant life of prosperity, you must uncover limiting beliefs like these, recognize they are toxic, and replace them with positive beliefs that serve and empower you. Uncover those limiting beliefs. Strip them down. Torch them if you must. Because the real surprise comes next—when you discover that prosperity is not what you think it is.

Chapter 5:

Prosperity Is Not What You Think

Okay, so far...

We've established that poverty sucks and there's nothing inherently noble or virtuous about it.

We've determined that living rich is a spiritual quest to be pursued.

Finally, we've come to grips with the reality that you didn't arrive at your current state by accident.

Before we get too much farther in this look at manifesting a prosperous life, we should take some time to break down what prosperity really means and how you go about manifesting it.

On second thought, it may be better to start with what prosperity is not.

Prosperity isn't greed, materialism, or the pursuit of shiny toys for the sake of ego. It's not a moral prize handed to the virtuous or a cosmic lottery that rewards random, lucky people.

Prosperity isn't about escaping struggle—it's about transcending it. It's not measured by what's parked in your driveway or hanging in your closet but by how much freedom, peace, and purpose you create in your life.

And let's be clear: poverty isn't noble, and playing small doesn't make you humble. That's counterfeit virtue sold by people who profit when you stay ignorant, sick, or broke.

True prosperity is not about having more than others. It's about refusing to settle for less than the greatness you are capable of.

At its essence, I believe prosperity is about freedom and self-determination. About living your life without self-created or externally applied artificial constraints.

Prosperity isn't about what you own—it's about who you become.

Prosperity is the freedom to grow into the highest possible version of yourself—physically, mentally, emotionally, and spiritually. When you live in that freedom, you experience prosperity through four essential quadrants:

1. Wellness

2. Resources

3. Harmony

4. Significance

Wellness shows up as vitality, confidence, and radiant health. Resources include money, time, and every tool that expands your possibilities. Harmony is your inner peace and your outer alignment—the relationships, values, and beliefs that keep you grounded. And Significance is the ultimate expression of prosperity: contribution, purpose, and legacy.

The 4 Quadrants of Prosperity

Wellness	Resources
· Energy · Self-Esteem · Health	· Money · Time · Your Network · Material Things
Harmony	**Significance**
· Inner Peace · Spiritual Sustenance · Healthy Relationships · Values	· Contribution · Purpose · Legacy

Everything else—financial success, meaningful work, love, adventure, growth—are simply how those four quadrants express themselves through you.

This creates an ever-expanding cycle of continuous increase in all areas, a "flywheel" if you will. Your health allows you to pursue new and exciting adventures that enhance your life and relationships. Your freedom of time allows you to increase the moments with the people who bring more joy into your life. Your money and assets are set up in platforms that cause them to produce more money and assets. You wake up every day wealthier than you were when you went to bed the night before. This increasing wealth allows you to buy back more of your time, which allows you to rinse and repeat everything just mentioned. Once this happens, you discover that…

The substance of all forms of true prosperity are infinite and, once manifested on the physical plane, create their own expansion.

This is demonstrated in all instances of prosperity manifestation, such as health, love, happiness, joy, and even money, because all forms of prosperity are boundless and infinite. The more you circulate, the more you receive back. This allows you to live in prosperity consciousness, amplifying who you are, giving you yet more freedom to grow and develop, and feeding the flywheel of ever-expanding prosperity.

The fact that so many people are ignorant on something as vital to the human condition as living a prosperous life is a crime against humanity. The principles that govern prosperity are demonstrated daily, so it's shocking how many people haven't got a clue about them. I think the concept of prosperity is complex, confusing, and indecipherable for many because there are too many hot takes and bad premises being bandied about on the subject.

In one camp, we have all the negative programming portraying money as evil and rich people as villains. In another camp we have those who suggest money isn't necessary for prosperity. And finally, there's another faction promoting only the hedonistic elements of money and material things as the end goal, completely ignoring the other necessary elements of prosperity. None of these viewpoints capture what I consider to be the true definition of a prosperous life.

When you have all four quadrants working at a high level,

that's when prosperity is achieved. This is a holistic condition involving every aspect of your life. It's not a truth to be learned but a way of living to participate in—a mindful state of existence.

Let's double-click on each of the quadrants...

Prosperity begins with Wellness. Living a prosperous life doesn't mean you never face adversity; it means you are better able to navigate challenges successfully when they occur. To do this, you need robust physical health and a beneficial thinking process. The longest-living people in the Blue Zones don't chase comfort; they seek wellness.

All things in the Universe at their ultimate level are energy vibrations, including you. To be prosperous, you need positive energy to pull you through each day. Even if you're getting chemo or lose a loved one, you can approach your circumstances with a positive mindset. This is a lot easier to do if you practice nourishing daily habits (eating, hydrating, exercising, and sleeping)—so you create a healthier mental state. This plays across all aspects of your life.

The *Resources* quadrant is where money and material things enter the chat. This begins with survival and security aspects. If your children aren't safe playing in the yard, your home is at risk of break-ins, or you don't have sufficient money for rent, food, or utilities, then your ability to live a prosperous life is seriously compromised. Studies show people with even a modest $500 emergency fund have dramatically reduced stress markers.

Moving down a level, there are many other elements that may

not technically be required for prosperity but radically impact it. Examples of this would be having enough financial clout to afford proper dental care, a safer automobile, and organic, healthy food. Toss in freedom from the indentured servitude of debt to this category as well. No one who is paying the minimum balance to the pawn shop or on their credit cards each month is living in prosperity.

And we can also admit that there are many other pleasures that can be experienced when you have greater resources. Things like booking the oceanfront room versus the dumpster-front room, buying the apartment on the higher floor with the better view, or treating yourself to a spa day after completing a difficult project aren't necessary for survival but certainly can enhance your life.

While we can say that the quality of your life can be determined when you're doing nothing, we should still acknowledge there's a difference between doing nothing in a roach-infested apartment and doing nothing in a penthouse. (Reminder: I'm speaking from firsthand experience.)

I labeled the third category Harmony because it encompasses the many spiritual, blissful, or transcendent aspects of a prosperous life. This shows up in different ways for different people. For some it is religious, others metaphysical, yet others secular. The one constant is an appreciation for the sacred gift of living in accordance with your true nature of yourself and vibrating in harmony with the environment around you. You're comfortable in your own skin, feel empathy toward others (including plants, animals, and solar systems), and work toward the greater good.

This includes many joyous, blissful, and magical things we can experience for free, but we must mindfully make time for. Walking in nature, noticing the clouds, or sharing a hug with someone you love, for example. It's important to slow down and rh these moments as they become available to you. Meditation research repeatedly shows improved emotional regulation for the people who practice it.

In this state of harmony, you recognize that all true forms of prosperity are infinite; others don't have to do without for you to have. You know that the more prosperity you circulate, the more prosperity will return to you. While good mental health is part of the wellness quadrant, overall peace of mind is represented in this one.

Please understand the distinction between happiness and harmony. Harmony does not mean that you're happy all the time, and this isn't a high you should attempt to chase. Even someone who lives a prosperous life will not be happy all the time. In fact, trying to be happy all the time ensures that you will never be happy.

We think happiness is when our team wins the Super Bowl, our friends remember our birthday, or we drink in a beautiful sunrise. But those events are just symptoms of the main dynamic, which is harmony.

There will always be people, events, and situations in life that will make you unhappy, and that's entirely natural. In fact, unhappiness might be the greatest gift life ever offers you. Most successful people will talk about a severe setback or failure in their earlier life that became a catalyst for their later success. And many of them will tell you that they were motivated by their substantial unhappiness when they were broke. Difficult situations that cause you harm, setbacks, or distress are supposed to suck.

Happy people are not always joyful, delighted, and blissful. They sometimes experience grief, get angry, and feel sad. This rainbow of emotions is normal; suppressing them is not healthy and it's okay (and necessary) to experience them. These are all part of the yin-yang dynamic that governs life. Once you learn how to process complex emotions like anxiety, fear, rage, and sadness, you can attain harmony. Once you make harmony your purpose, it's the kind of magnetic goal that pulls you toward it.

The way this shows up (when you're in your harmony sweet spot) is what I've quantified as:

The Seven Elements of an Abundant Life

1. Do work that lights you up.
2. Collaborate only with people who share your unbridled passion for the work.
3. Operate at peak-level energy and wellness.
4. Enjoy healthy, positive, and elevating relationships.
5. Get the money thing out of the way.
6. Seek each day to move toward the highest possible version of yourself.
7. Make the transition from success to significance.

These aren't bullet points; they're a daily prosperity mindset checklist. Lived expressions of alignment. By the way, you can download a free booklet about the seven elements on the homepage of my website: https://randygage.com/)

The *Significance* quadrant is the one where vital concepts like meaning, purpose, contribution, and challenge factor heavily. (Which we'll explore deeper in Chapter Fourteen.) Meaning and purpose are readily apparent to most people. They understand that simply chasing money, accomplishments, recognition, status, or acceptance is a recipe for a shallow, superficial life.

The singular pursuit of cash at some point leads to the Pablo Escobar result. You employ money-counting machines to bundle your banknotes into shrink-wrapped pallets of cash that fill entire semi-trucks—or the modern equivalent of cryptocurrency in cold storage—but live a miserable existence only to die in regret. (Fun fact: At its height, the Medellín Cartel was smuggling $1.8 billion worth of cocaine a month into the U. S.—and spending $4,000 a month on rubber bands to bundle their cash.)

If you just chase money, this can lead you to a life as unfulfilling and bleak as Escobar's, only without the helicopters and hippos. (Although you'll spend a lot less on rubber bands.)

As we said earlier, money and prosperity are inextricably intertwined. But as your prosperity evolves, you will appreciate that success isn't nearly as rewarding as significance; you want to know that what you do makes a difference. Virtually every major study on life satisfaction (and literally every single one I've seen) ranks contribution and service above wealth.

The missing element in this quadrant for many people is the challenge aspect. It seems ironic, but having everything go your way all the time is depressing. Iron sharpens iron and facing some friction along the way is necessary for growth.

(And growth is required for sustained contentment.)
To manifest prosperity, you not only have to embrace challenge but actively seek it, knowing that it is your steppingstone to enlightenment. Challenges force you to become the person you need to become—to achieve what you truly desire.

At the risk of being branded as a drunken metaphysical poet, allow me to opine like a drunken metaphysical poet: True prosperity happens once you become a figurative cauldron with ingredients of these four quadrants sloshing around in concentric relativity, ebbing and flowing with the energy transference between you and the Universe around you. The power comes not from one quadrant or another, but the symbiotic synergy created by the whole formula.

Living in accord with the four quadrants produces a life that is an intoxicating mélange of challenge, adventure, and growth.

Quick reflection: Which of the four quadrants are you currently the strongest in? Which one sucks the most energy from you? Allow me to suggest writing down one action this week to restore balance before reading on.

Prosperity isn't a goal—it's a state of being. And your mind is either amplifying it…or short-circuiting it. If your outer world isn't changing fast enough, it's because your inner wiring hasn't caught up yet.

Let's fix that…

Chapter 6:

Rewire Your Mind—Before It Bankrupts You

If you hacked my laptop, these are the types of questions you'd find in my DMs and email:

Both my spouse and I have great jobs, we're high-income earners with retirement security taken care of, but we live like paupers. How can I get him (her) to relax and spend money on things like travel and vacations?

Did I self-sabotage my promotion because of subconscious programming I received about money when I was seven?

How do I break my cycle of repeating toxic relationships?

I'm hustling, grinding, and working my face off, but I can't get any real traction to break the million-dollar ceiling. What's holding me back?

Did I blow up my marriage because of worthiness issues I

developed from my religious beliefs?

I have a hugely successful business, fly private, and own all the toys. But my marriage is in shambles and my health is even worse. WTF do I do?

If you've ever struggled with questions like these, this is your book. If you've ever struggled to apply the timeless first principles of prosperity in a world of identity politics, social media manipulation, and toxic polarization, this is your book.

When you live your daily life with prosperity consciousness, you bend the Universe to your will. Really. Nothing woo-woo about that, simply physics. At the ultimate level, everything in the Universe is energy vibrations. And energy can be either attracted or repelled. You either attract the people and circumstances that manifest health, happiness, and prosperity into your life or you repel them.

Because:

- How you talk to yourself is how the world is going to talk with you.
- How you treat yourself is how the world is going to treat you.
- How you value yourself determines how the world values you.

And it goes the other way as well. Because:

- How you talk to yourself determines how you talk to your spouse, your kids, and the gate agent when your flight is delayed.
- How you treat yourself determines how you treat the waitress, elderly people, and the puppy who tries to gnaw

on your ankle.

- How you value yourself determines how much you value music, civility, poetry, empathy, kindness, other people, and life itself.

The ripple *effects* go on and on and on…

It may sound corny or even grandiose to you, but as you see above, you really do have the power to alter the trajectory of the Universe, even if only a few millimeters. When you transform your consciousness, you transform your life. And when you transform your life, you transform other lives.

The Ripple Effect

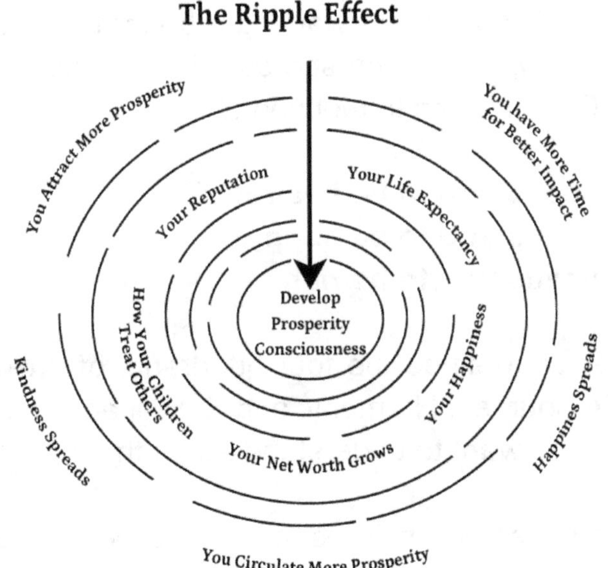

I'm old enough to remember a time when the prevalent wisdom was that the surest, safest path to "prosperity" meant lowering your expectations and desires. (Probably because that time was last week.) The world we live in doesn't require that any longer. And probably never did.

You're living in the most abundant time in human history. You weren't born to be broke, stressed, or apologizing for wanting more out of your life. In fact, quite the opposite. You were born to seek, desire, and expand. Abundance is your natural state.

So why do so many smart, capable people stay trapped in lack, riddled with guilt, and playing so small?

They've been brainwashed for mediocrity. Ridiculed for dreaming big. Chastised for wanting a better life. If you want to live a healthy, happy, prosperous life, all that nonsense stops now. Did I happen to mention…

The world needs you to be healthy.
The world needs you to be happy.
The world needs you to be rich.

Last chapter we defined the four quadrants of prosperity of Wellness, Resources, Harmony, and Significance. But here's something you'll want to understand about that…

Prosperity is not simply the presence of Wellness, Resources, Harmony, and Significance. Prosperity is a state of consciousness.

Likewise…

Poverty is not simply the absence of Wellness, Resources, Harmony, and Significance. Poverty is also a state of consciousness.

Both consciousnesses are created by your perspective—the window through which you view the world. In Chapter Four we discussed the process of programming creating beliefs, those beliefs creating a vision, that vision creating habits, and those habits creating your reality. Whatever reality you've created determines the size of that window you see the world through.

Many people looked at Amazon stock in the early days and decided it was a poor risk, while others saw an untapped behemoth waiting to emerge. Exact same company. The difference was the size of the window each group saw the world through.

Perhaps you and another person were applying for the same job at a company. When it came time to ask what salary you wanted, you asked for $80,000 and the other person might have said $120,000. The job is the same. The difference is the size of your windows. (P.S. The person who asks for a larger salary is usually the one who gets hired.)

There is no way to prosperity. Prosperity is the way.

What I mean by that is all the things we discuss throughout the book are contingent on your seeing the world through a bigger window with prosperity consciousness instead of poverty consciousness.

- You can meet your perfect soulmate, but if you have poverty consciousness, you'll blow up the relationship.

- You can sign a $400 million contract with the LA Dodgers, but if you have poverty consciousness, you'll probably end up with a PED suspension that voids the deal.
- You can win a billion-dollar lotto jackpot, but if you have poverty consciousness, you'll likely wind up broke again.

"For as he thinks in his heart, so is he."
From just that one sentence in the Book of Proverbs, James Allen was able to write at least five profound books. That's a lot of work from ten little words, but it speaks to how powerful the idea they convey really is. Because whatever you constantly think about, not only will you come to understand, but you will become. You grow into the likeness of your thoughts. Those thoughts become integral to your very being and become your very Self.

Tell me what it is that you most frequently and intensely think about in your silent hours, and I will tell you the path of peace or pain you are traveling.

Big Pharma hasn't been able to create a Prosperity Ozempic. As a result, you can't be treated for prosperity—you must be open to receiving it. If you're operating from poverty consciousness, you'll self-sabotage any form of prosperity you begin to manifest. So, it's important to take some time to sketch out the mental and physical states you must be in to open yourself up to receive the prosperity that is your birthright.

To create a baseline of prosperity consciousness you need a mindset default setting toward harmony, positivity, and optimism. Which can certainly seem difficult when you're worried about making the payroll or feeding your family.

But even in the most challenging situations, things can (and must) be viewed with a perspective of the hidden benefits and gifts that can come from them. And the biggest contributor to this positive mental state begins with a physical state that allows you to get there. Let's explore some important physical habits that will produce a healthy, happy, and prosperous mental state.

Get adequate sleep. There is too much bad advice these days about grinding and hustling. There's a place for those things, particularly when you're young and just starting out. You have less money, fewer connections, limited other resources, and often must outwork your competitors to get ahead. I get it, but way too many people are still doing this in their forties and fifties. Just know this: The less you sleep, the less productive you are in the time you have for building prosperous outcomes.

My philosophy is that alarm clocks are inherently unhealthy, and your goal should be to wake up each morning when you finish sleeping. If you aren't waking up early enough to get to your obligations on time, this means you're not going to bed early enough. It might take a few weeks to adjust to a healthy routine, but it will pay dividends in all areas of your life.

Do cardio on every day that ends in "y." Seriously. If you live the normal sedentary lifestyle, you'll eventually devolve into someone who needs help getting out of a chair or is unable to climb five steps. You need cardiovascular exercise every day to oxygenate your blood and keep your lungs and heartbeat strong. (Which keeps your thinking strong.)

Perform resistance training at least two or three times a week. You need a good muscle-to-fat ratio to burn off excess fat that threatens your life. And muscles that aren't used will atrophy. You need a regular routine that works for you. If you can afford to hire a personal trainer, great. If not, a quick search on YouTube or Instagram will reveal the help you need.

Eat and drink clean. Here's something you can count on: You are going to be assaulted daily with literally hundreds of messages attempting to brainwash you into consuming food and drink that ranges from little or no nutritional value to stuff that is outright dangerous for your health. Create a proactive, clean, eating plan built around mindful shopping, preparation, and dining out.

The actions above will allow your physical body to best support your thinking process. Next, you're going to want to do some work to specifically elevate your mindset. Some of this work is adding by subtraction.

There are three aspects of modern life that pose immense danger to your prosperity consciousness:
- Smartphone addiction

- Social media

- Toxic people (who likely became that way in large part because of the first two)

Neuroscientists have now shown that constant digital stimulation lowers your attention span and increases your reactivity—which is pretty much the opposite of a prosperous mental state. I could start doing footnotes here and linking to scientific study after scientific study on smartphone effects. But let me give you my tl;dr version that even a braindead moron on crack will know to be true…

I'd guess that 95 percent of humans with smartphones are addicted to them. They check them constantly—in every elevator, at each red light, during the countless commercials on TV, and in between bites of their meals. As a result, they develop the attention span of a gnat on a double Espresso. They lose the ability for focus, mindful reflection, and clarity. These abilities are indispensable for mental harmony.

Ninety percent of people are using their cellphone in bed before they go to sleep. It's been proven that phone screens affect your circadian rhythms and disrupt your sleep, making you sleepier the next day. Even worse is what you're getting exposed to during that viewing. Most of this is negative news, contrived controversy, and sensationalism. A lot of it is mindless social media doom scrolling. These platforms have spent billions of dollars developing algorithms to trigger you into fear, rage, and jealousy. Online marketers spend billions more making you feel less than, so you are more motivated to buy the stuff they want to sell you.

Go to sleep reactively and you're guaranteed to wake up reactively. There is a direct correlation between the time you spend on your phone in bed and the reduction in your productivity, happiness, and prosperity the following day.

No child under sixteen should be allowed on a social media platform. Adults would be smart to avoid these platforms entirely as well. If I weren't an author, there's not a chance in hell I would be on any on them. If you do find them helpful for business, I recommend my approach: I'm a content creator but not a consumer. And the single best piece of prosperity advice I can give you is to unplug from your phone at least a couple hours before bedtime and charge it in a room you're not sleeping in.

Thomas Edison advised to never go to bed without a request to your subconscious. Imagine what happens when you do that instead of digesting the latest polarizing, otherizing, demonizing debate on social media or TV.

You can paint me as the cranky old man screaming at the kids to stay off his lawn, but ignore this advice at your peril. I adamantly believe that for most people, the time they are spending on their screens and social media is murdering their prosperity consciousness.

Perhaps the most important part of mental health and mindset is the people who you allow to speak into your life. **The fastest route to prosperity consciousness is surrounding yourself with people who challenge you to become a higher version of yourself.** Jim Rohn famously said that your income will be the average income of the five people you spend the most time with. I'll take it further and suggest it applies to your health, relationships, and mental harmony as well.
If you are on a path of growth and enlightenment—it's likely you will have to upgrade the people in your inner circle a few times in your life.

This isn't about being arrogant, mean-spirited, or thinking you're better than others. It's recognizing that everyone is at different stages of their journey and wanting the highest good for all involved. People grow and reach awareness at different speeds and different levels.

Recognizing this, you realize there are some people you need to start lowering your exposure to. Maybe instead of meeting for dinner once a week, you change to every other week or once a month. There may be groups, or social events, or specific environments that you decide to reduce your participation with. And it must be said that there are some people—a good friend, a family member, or even a spouse—who are so toxic that they are a threat to your health and safety. You must remove them from your life completely. (Are you thinking of anyone like that right now?)

Mindfully work to find and attract people who are operating at a higher consciousness. Spend more time with them. Invite those people into your life and think about how you can add value to theirs.

Once you step back from your smartphone addiction, social media brainwashing, and spending too much time with toxic people, you create a vacuum, one you can fill with people, activities, and resources that provide positive, prosperous input.

Most people have a continuous tug-of-war going on between their conscious and subconscious minds. They have a conscious desire to become wealthy and successful, while at the same time they have subconscious programming that rich people are evil. Something's gotta give for you to create a harmonious life.

Even if you have been mindfully working to develop prosperity consciousness, you've probably fallen prey to some of the hundreds of anti-wealth messages you get assaulted with every day of your life.

Here's a quick reality check for you: If you didn't notice and think about at least five negative mind viruses you received today, then odds are you were reinfected with more negative memes about money and success.

Did you consciously notice even one thing today—a joke about rich jerks, a snarky comment about successful people, or perhaps a plot in a TV show portraying a wealthy person in an evil way? If you didn't, I suggest you up your daily counterprogramming of positive messaging.

Even if you strive not to be, you are going to be exposed to hundreds of negative, judgmental messages about money, material things, and being successful every day. And if they aren't sounding an alarm on your radar—you are being programmed with them.

You should be furious at all the people, companies, and institutions that are emotionally manipulating you to do what they want you to do and buy what they want you to buy. And after you're done being furious, you'd better get focused, determined, and resourceful. You're going to have to get smarter, become a critical thinker, and recognize the programming you're receiving and counterprogram against it. Because only when you operate in a state of prosperity consciousness can you manifest a prosperous life.

And believe it or not, that awakening doesn't start with adding anything new…

It starts with removing what no longer serves you. In other words…you begin by creating a vacuum.

Chapter 7:

Create a Vacuum the Universe Has to Fill

One evening after a prosperity seminar, one of my students walked up to me confused. She had been attending the classes for weeks and questioned how "all this prosperity stuff" could be working, since she had recently lost both her job and her boyfriend. To me, the answer was pretty obvious but required taking her through a thinking process to bring some insights to the surface...

She had been complaining about that job for months. Her pay was lousy and there seemed to be no room for advancement. Several times during the class she had discussed her boyfriend being both physically and verbally abusive to her.

Without even realizing it, she had manifested the first step to her prosperity breakthrough: creating a vacuum.

As her consciousness developed, her job could no longer hold her, and her boyfriend was no longer comfortable with her. (Because he could no longer control her.) Ultimately, she found a fulfilling job with much higher wages and attracted a great guy who appreciated her and provided the human dignity that is the birthright of us all. Had she clung to what she had instead of creating a vacuum, she would likely never have manifested the better results in her life.

People frequently complain about the circumstances they're fighting but don't practice any critical thinking about what they are doing to create or contribute to those circumstances. If you and I were hanging out with James Allen at the local coffee shop, he would likely ask, "What's the point of fighting an effect, all the while you are nourishing and preserving the cause that is in your heart?"

That cause could be a conscious vice like alcohol, other drugs, or a gambling addiction. Or an unconscious belief like thinking you're not worthy, money is bad, it's spiritual to be poor, you must sell your soul for money, or other dysfunctional premises. Unless and until you deal with the cause, the effect is going to keep coming back.

The Universe fills vacuums. And since the inherent nature of the Universe is progressive, a vacuum will ultimately be filled with a positive result. When you walk along the beach, you leave footprints in the sand. But give the wind and the waves enough time and those tracks will be filled.

The Universe can't put anything in your hand until you let go of what you're grasping. This takes us back to the vacuum dynamic and how you can unknowingly choke off the prosperity you're meant to enjoy...

Holding on to a negative belief will often prevent you from recognizing and accepting the prosperity you deserve. When you're not manifesting prosperity in all areas of your life, the first question to ask is...

"What am I holding on to that I need to release?"

In other words, find where you need to create a vacuum.

How are you going to manifest your ideal soulmate if you're holding on to an abusive current relationship that you think is right for you?

How will you manifest optimal health if you hold on to the false programming you receive every time you watch a commercial from a fast-food restaurant?

How will you become wealthy if you're still harboring a belief that rich people are evil?

There's an infinite number of ways you can create a vacuum...

- If you want more energy, remove all the junk food from your cupboards.
- If you want some new shoes, clean out your closet and donate some old ones to the homeless shelter.
- If you want more mental harmony, add a "no devices day" to your calendar each week.
- If you want yet more mental harmony, delete social media apps from your phone.

- If you want more happiness in your life, let go of any religious doctrines or dogma that teach you are unworthy.
- If you want to be more productive, clean up the clutter around you.
- If you want more prosperity consciousness in your life, reduce the time spent with people who pull you down.

There is an epidemic of entitlement and victimhood-thinking in the world today. And now there are industries spending trillions of dollars training AI algorithms to weaponize your negative and limiting beliefs against you. You get brainwashed to eat stuff that's killing you and doom scroll for hours on platforms that are turning you into a raging lunatic.

The greatest beneficial impact of applying the vacuum dynamic in your life is letting go of the beliefs that don't serve you. This creates a vacuum to attract good.

If you are holding on to being a victim...there is no space in your mind to become a victor.

Once you let go of your victimhood, a whole new world of possibilities opens for you. Health challenges resolve, relationships improve, your finances get better, and your happiness skyrockets. Nothing external changes. The change is created within you. Which triggers the behaviors that lead to better results in all areas of your life.

No doubt...it takes a certain amount of faith to practice this law. *You must be willing to let go of jobs, beliefs, even people close to you.* That can be scary. In my own case, I gather faith from the way the Universe unfolds. The weakest members of the herd are culled, stronger DNA prevails, organisms innovate for survival, forest fires reduce dead vegetation to fuel growth, etc.

Natural Selection. Natural Subtraction.

These vacuums are all part of the evolutionary progression of the Universe. Once you realize that the Universe is inherently good, it is easier to have faith in prosperous outcomes. You no longer fear releasing things, because you know that they will be replaced with something of equal or even greater value.

You are surrounded by a Universe of good everywhere. (No matter what the media tries to get you to believe.) The only lack is the lack in your mind. But you can't simply watch *The Secret* and expect your new Bentley to roll up in the driveway. Because prosperity rewards players, not spectators. You have to step onto the field. So let's talk about the money game—and how to win it.

82

Chapter 8:

How to Play—and Win—the Money Game

"If I lost it all tomorrow and had to start all over, I would be a millionaire again within two years."

I used to proclaim that statement above with great pride. Not only did I swell with superiority when I said it, but I proved it. Twice.

You might be thinking I'm sharing that experience with you to illustrate the mental side of the prosperity equation, or perhaps it's a flex to demonstrate my cred in the prosperity arena. While I love a flex as much as the next Neanderthal, I'm sharing that story with you to demonstrate a hard lesson I learned through the process.

Unfortunately, the tutorial was on what a dumb fucking moron (DFM) I was. *Please. Don't be a DFM. I was dumb enough for the both of us.*

Recently I made the following post on my social media channels:

True or False?
If money can solve your problems, you don't have any real problems.

About 60 percent of the people replying selected false. As the prosperity teacher, I marked their answers wrong. Because I believe you can always manifest more money with the right idea. This means that no one actually has a money shortage; what they really suffer from is an idea shortage. Therefore, if you have a problem that can be solved with more money, it simply means that you haven't developed the necessary idea to make the perceived problem go away.

You already know that money is not the sole determiner of prosperity. And I've already warned you that this isn't a money or finance book. But the better choices that money can provide you are such a vital element of the journey toward prosperity, I felt you would immensely benefit from a special chapter on how the money game works and what it takes for you to win it.

Coming from the poverty consciousness of my early years, once I discovered how to earn large amounts of money, I foolishly assumed I had the money game figured out. But that was exactly what the people who run the game wanted me (and now want you) to think.

Just as rats don't know that someone built the maze, most of us don't realize that the money system is a game. But it is.

A very complex game which is rigged against you by a long list of villains:

- Banks
- Credit Card Companies
- Financial Planning Firms
- Cable Finance Networks
- Investment Advisors
- Governments
- Insurance Carriers
- Mobile Payment Apps
- Financial Publishing Houses
- Money Influencers

These institutions are branded and positioned in a way that makes them appear to be your trusted allies and advisors in your prosperity journey. (And many of the people employed in those industries are kind, loving, and mean well.) But most of those institutions have a vested interest in making sure you continue operating as a worker-cog in the collective.

- You might train yourself how to get by on five hours of sleep and pursue the "grinder/hustle/coffee is for closers" routines that are mainstays on many podcasts today. You will still probably end up unhappy, unhealthy, and unwealthy.

- You could discover the right crypto shitcoin at the exact right time, ride it to the moon, and sell just before it craters. You will still probably end up unhappy, unhealthy, and unwealthy.

- You may even hit the pick-six in the lotto or inherit a fortune from a rich relative. You will still probably end up unhappy, unhealthy, and unwealthy.

The problem each of the scenarios above share is they are all predicated on the same bad premise: The money game was designed so you can win it. But it's exactly the opposite. You're playing a money game against the institutions that created the rules so you would lose. They change the rules at their whim, and you don't even know what those rules are.

It's time you learn how to play and win that game.

Before we get to specifics, remember these two vital instructions:

1. Always question the source. (Including me. Especially me. I was expelled from high school FFS. What could I possibly know about wealth building that the financial geniuses on CNBC don't?)
2. Always question the premise.

In my case, I've never watched more than ten minutes of financial cable networks and haven't read an investing publication in years. (Full disclosure: Back when I was broke, I read the WSJ, Forbes, Fortune, and Investor's Business Daily religiously.)

I couldn't care less where the Dow, NASDAQ, or S&P 500 are at, and if my very life depended on it, I could not tell you the difference between a bear market, a bull market, or a seafood market. Not only is that data irrelevant to me, but I believe it's often dangerous. The source of most of that data is the bad actors above. The premise of most of that data is that it's being provided to help you make sound financial decisions for your highest good. And if you believe that, I have some oceanfront property in Wisconsin I want to sell you...

The money ecosystem is infested with a high percentage of predatory people and institutions. Even many of the well-meaning people are ignorant of how the game is played themselves and are simply disseminating the herd-thinking mind viruses they've been infected with.

A friend once asked me if *Rich Dad Poor Dad* was my number-one go-to book about growing wealth. The poor bloke was almost traumatized when I replied that book wouldn't make my top one hundred money manuscripts. Fun fact: I came thiiiis close to titling this book, No Dad, Poor Mom. Not to throw shade on Kiyosaki, because his book is a great one containing many helpful lessons about building wealth.

Those lessons simply weren't accessible to me when I first read Kiyosaki's book, because the reason I was broke wasn't because I didn't understand about building assets. I was broke because I was riddled with subconscious programming—that I had no idea was in there—to believe I didn't deserve good things. Along with another entire layer of beliefs that rich people were jackasses and poor people were noble.

I believe most people today need to go through the same process of discovering and destroying limiting beliefs that are keeping them unhealthy, sad, and broke. Only then can you apply the financial principles you might learn from Kiyosaki, Suze Orman, or Dave Ramsey.

If that's you, this is your book.

What you're reading are the lessons I've learned in the real world: selling dope in middle school, starting and exiting companies, waiting tables at Red Lobster, serving as a strategic advisor to some of the brightest CEOs and founders on Earth, having my restaurant seized by the tax authorities, and producing more than $23 billion in revenues for myself, clients, and protégées.

My journey from washing dishes in a pancake house to earning a spot in the wealthiest one percent had potholes, speed bumps, and detours along the way, but it provided some fascinating insights on how the money game is played by the people who win it. Allow me to take you behind the curtain and reveal how to protect yourself against the bad guys, create some positive financial movement forward, and end up where you're meant to be: healthy, happy, and prosperous.

Like most worthy endeavors, building your financial freedom is less about mysterious secrets and more about disciplined, common-sense behaviors. So, let's not overthink this. Here are seven simple yet profound premises I'm going to build my case around:

1. Your goal is to wake up each morning wealthier than when you went to sleep.
2. You don't have to be an investor or insider to grow your wealth, just financially literate.
3. An employee can create wealth, but I believe entrepreneurs can do it bigger, easier, and faster.
4. Don't seek financial advice from broke people.
5. You never go broke from the deal you didn't do.
6. Either you're using leverage or someone is using you for leverage.

7. Don't be a DFM.

As mentioned earlier, don't be afraid to question a premise. I believe the seven premises presented above will withstand the scrutiny and ground you in a strong financial foundation.

To win the money game requires you to understand a few simple but extremely significant wealth-building concepts. Let's run through them…

Prosperity Begins by Knowing the Truth.

Begin by knowing some of your metrics, and one of the most important ones is your net worth. Which, if you're like most people, is likely negative. You might have high levels of debt and not have any financial assets working for you. Whatever it is, it is, but you need to know the truth.

Please don't be discouraged if you are in a negative state. It's not about where you start but where you end up. Just facing the truth and developing awareness of your current situation will put you ahead of virtually 70 percent of the population. (Most of those people posting pics of their new ride or luxurious vacation on your social media feed are doing it with debt and are still in denial.)

For you, a huge part of the battle is already won because you're lowering your level of ignorance. And this is a textbook case of how knowledge can become power as you use this information in the following chapter on getting out of debt. Please don't beat yourself up. On the contrary, give yourself a pat on the back because you're still here learning.

Beat Your Burn Rate.

You've heard you should spend less than what you earn at least a million times and know it's true. So why don't more people practice this? Because they allow themselves to be brainwashed into an instant-gratification lifestyle. If you're spending everything you're taking in, you're going to get hammered at some point by a job loss, personal emergency, or economic meltdown of some kind. This won't have a happy ending.

Worse, if you're like most people and spend more than you earn—and financing the excess with debt—you're building your own prison. This situation has an even unhappier ending. You're receiving hundreds of messages daily, all designed to seduce you into buying things you don't need, with money you don't have, to impress people who don't matter…and who don't really care about you. Or buying things you may need but wouldn't be prudent to buy in your current financial situation. Be willing to sacrifice early to luxuriate later.

Discipline = freedom.

Think about your wealth creation activities with a similar philosophy to the one that venture capital and angel investors use. Two important metrics they look at first are the burn rate and the runway. The burn rate simply means the regular monthly expenses: the amount of money that is burned through each month to keep the doors open. The runway is the length of time before the venture will run out of money and shut down.

For a simple example, let's suppose you have a company

funded with $200,000 to begin. The amount of your rent, taxes, payroll, travel, etc., is $10,000 a month. With that burn rate of 10k a month, your runway would be twenty months.

Now apply those concepts to you and your personal finances. Mentally picture yourself as a company: You, Inc.

You have a certain financial footprint required to live each month. This includes expenses such as your rent or mortgage, maintenance fees, groceries, auto upkeep, and utilities. Make sure you include things that occur only occasionally or annually, like health care, gym memberships, insurance, and income taxes. And don't forget about expenditures that aren't essential but you're making anyway, like cable or streaming services, hobbies, and vacations.

Take the time to do this right. Progress won't begin until you're dealing with the reality of how you live. Then you need to calculate how much you owe. Every credit card balance, installment plan, amount outstanding on your home and car, etc. This is another area where progress won't happen unless you're telling yourself the truth. (Years ago, I fought taking the time to list what my own credit card debt was, figuring I knew the ballpark amount was almost 100k. That thought was depressing enough that I didn't want to pick the scab any deeper. Imagine the jolt when I finally did the math and discovered I had $180k in credit card balances. Some of which were at interest rates around 30 percent. More about this in a bit.)

Beating your burn rate means you take in more money each month than you pay out. If you're spending as much or more than what you earn, it must stop now. (If you're not willing to make this change, no need to read further. Seriously, if you're not fervently committed to spending less than you earn: STOP HERE. Go back to the beginning and re-read this book…more slowly and thoughtfully this time. If you get to this point the second time and you're still not willing to do the math about your spending and commit to spending less than you earn… don't waste any more time…you're not ready.)

Either take on a part-time job or business to produce some extra income or make the hard decisions of what you can eliminate to reduce your burn rate. (Or do both!)

The goal is to get your burn rate to the point where you have some money left for investing in wealth-producing platforms. Think of this fund as your retirement or financial freedom investment pool—providing you security and working for you when you sleep. Because…this pool must not only protect you from a financial calamity but, more importantly, also be building your wealth.

Imagine a place in your future where work is optional. You don't have to stop working…but could if you wanted to. You would know that a portion of your total assets—your financial net worth—will generate all the after-tax spending money that you want to fund your ideal lifestyle as long as you could possibly live.

The speed with which your investment pool is building your worth is important as well. Your wealth needs to appreciate at a rate greater than that of inflation created by the financially illiterate people who govern us. Do not trust your financial security to your government. That's like hiring Hannibal Lecter to do your grocery shopping and finding out you're the entrée.

Most public policy in finance is created by people who hold degrees in economics but know nothing about building wealth. They are upside down on their BMW leases, making payments on their dining room sets, and saddled with credit card debt. The laws they propose come from the lobbyists hired by the banks, credit card companies, financial publishers, etc.

You Work for Money…or Money Works for You.

It sounds simplistic, but the previous sentence may be the most profound statement ever written on creating prosperity. You may want to print it out and post it above your computer or on your bathroom mirror.

YOU WORK FOR MONEY…OR MONEY WORKS FOR YOU.

Taking this to the next level, for the most part, broke people work for money and wealthy people have money work for them. This means if you're serious about moving from broke to wealthy, you must take a percentage of your income and put it to work making money, so you unleash the awesome power of leverage and compounding.

Put another way, make sure that while you are working for money that you are making enough and living within your means so you can put as much money as possible to work for you. That way, one day your having to work can be optional. It could be because you choose to stop working or because something goes sideways and forces you to stop working, but either way, you're covered.

Don't look for loopholes and don't make excuses. People all

the time tell me things like, "I can't get by on 100 percent of what I make. How can I survive on 90 percent?" Don't be a DFM. In the world of creating wealth, there's an important philosophy to live by:

When you make hard decisions, you create an easy life. If you make easy decisions, you'll end up with a hard life.

The non-leveraged model is simple; it's what most of the world does. They trade hours for money. Thus, their earning power is restricted by how many hours of productive work they can physically produce. In terms of creating wealth, this is the very worst strategy to employ, no matter how rewarding the hourly rate may be. A pilot earns an extremely lucrative hourly rate, but she can be out-earned by any sixteen-year-old who understands leverage and has a TikTok store.

The leveraged model looks simple as well, but when you look under the hood, it is quite profound. Because leverage allows you to transcend the limitations of space and time...

You can leverage your money. You might put down only $200,000 and buy a $1 million apartment building, which would leverage your earning power.

You can leverage your labor. Instead of mowing ten lawns a day, you can hire ten workers who each mow ten lawns a day, again leveraging your earning power.

You can leverage your time and effort. If you join a direct selling company and sponsor and train a dozen people, then teach them how to duplicate your results, you can build an organization that produces thousands of hours of productivity every week.

There are some limitations to these models because you are still dependent on others. You will need people who are willing to loan you money, work for you, or believe in your leadership abilities. Nevertheless, anytime you can apply leverage, you're much better off than the non-leverage model of trading hours for money.

Even when you can't access leverage by the models above, you can still use other approaches. You might drive for a ride share company, trading hours for money…but set aside that extra money and put it to work through leverage.

Remember: *You work for money or money works for you. Choose wisely.*

Convert Income Into Working Capital.

This is where we get into the officially sexy part of prosperity building. Because the sexiest part isn't earning but unleashing the power of leverage with your earnings. (Maybe that's why they call it capitalism instead of "workism.") Even if you're a movie star earning $10 million a film, if that's all you're doing… you're still trapped trading hours for money. Leverage is a superpower for building prosperity, because now your capital can earn money, even when you're sleeping.

Generate Steady Gains to Unleash Compounding.

Your initial goal is to beat your burn rate. Once you're doing that, you invest the surplus cash, then that capital starts producing gains, which you then reinvest into creating more and larger gains, using the principle of compounding. Now you're leveraging your leverage. This is when you create an ongoing cycle of increasing wealth that allows you to achieve the perfect outcome: waking up every morning wealthier than you were when you went to sleep the night before.

Utilize Smart Debt, Avoid DFM Debt.

If you borrow $400,000 and use it to buy an income-producing property that provides positive cash flow while increasing your net worth, you are a genius. If you borrow $400 to upgrade your TV to a new OLED model, you are a DFM. And you don't want to be a DFM.

The goal is to eliminate foolish debt as fast as possible, because debt isn't just a number on a spreadsheet; it's a psychological prison. Learn to use debt wisely, and it becomes leverage. Let's talk next about which version you're creating…

Chapter 9:

Leverage or Landmine? The Truth About Debt

As we wrapped up the last chapter, you discovered there are two types of debt:

- Smart debt, which allows you to leverage your earning ability.

- Foolish debt, such as instant gratification purchases or financing imprudent, unnecessary, or reckless consumption.

Running up debt of the foolish kind is one of the most serious threats to your prosperity. It makes no sense to invest $1,000 that is getting you a six or eight percent return trying to grow wealth, while you have $30,000 in credit card debt on which you're getting zinged interest of 27 percent. If you're completely debt-free, you're in the driver's seat to start exponentially increasing your net worth. If you still are holding some foolish debt, then your next step is creating your…

Get Out of Foolish Debt Plan…

Nothing kills your prosperity faster than letting borrowed money own you. Your credit cards, car loan, mortgage…they all quietly drain your energy, dim your selfworth, and shut the door on abundance. Let's kick that door open.

Step 1: Get the Naked Truth

- You can't fix what you won't face.
- Pull every statement you've got: credit cards, store cards, car loans, personal loans—everything.
- List every balance, every interest rate, every minimum payment.
- Make a master list. Give yourself no hiding places.
- Find the debts that are bleeding you worst (highest rates). These are your priority targets.

Step 2: Make a Cold, Clear Promise (No Emotion, Full Strategy)

Emotion will kill this plan. Clarity saves it.

- Decide: "I WILL pay off the worst debt first." Then track monthly by line item, including minimums on all others plus extra on the highest rate.
- Commit: No new bad debt. Stop adding to the hole.
- If a card tempts you—the fine points matter: late fees, cash advances, penalty rates—kill the temptation. Cancel the card or freeze it.
- Don't revolve balances. Use cash or use only what you know you can pay off immediately.

Step 3: Negotiate & Disrupt the Terms

You don't have to be a victim of high interest. Money isn't always fixed; there is leverage.

- Call every creditor with interest over 12 percent. Tell them you're shopping balance transfer offers and better rates elsewhere. Ask if they will lower your APR. Many will do this on the spot, simply because you took the time to call and ask.

- Consider balance transfers if they make sense. If one card is charging 25 to 30 percent and someone else is offering five to six percent (or even zero interest) for twelve to eighteen months, that's a golden window. Use it. But don't use it as a crutch to just delay the problem.

- Watch out for fine print: skipped payments, deferred interest, an increase after promotional period. Know what you're stepping into.

Step 4: Kill Consumer Debt, Smartly Buy Big Treasures

Some debts are worse than others. But all debt that doesn't serve you is dangerous.

- Cars: Never buy a new car while you're upside-down on the old one. That negative spread gets thrown into the financing of your next car, and you pay multiple intertest on that money.

- If you need a car before you're debtfree, buy "almost new" or "gently used." Use warranties. Check histories, condition. Avoid high depreciation.

- Homes and mortgages: same principle—don't let debt for these things cripple you. Buy within your means. If you can pay cash without wiping out your life, do it. If not, structure so you're not living in financial fear. Consider getting a shorter loan structure.

Step 5: Build a Budget That Ignites, Not Inhibits

A budget isn't about deprivation; it's about direction.

- Set a real budget for your life. Food. Holidays. Gifts. Entertainment. Do this ahead of time.
- Every dollar "saved" goes toward your debtkill fund. Then when those debts expire, redirect that same cash toward something that builds you up (wealth, giving, significance).

Step 6: Celebrate Progress & Keep the Motivation Alive

You will need emotional fuel to stay in this fight.

- Celebrate each debt paid off. Big or small. That's momentum.
- Visualize being debt-free. What would your life feel like? What doors would open? Let that vision burn in you.
- Daily reminders: affirmations, journaling, mirror work (yes, mirror work even for money stuff). You are not a debtor; you are becoming debtfree.

Step 7: Shift from DebtAvoidant to WealthProactive

Once you've removed bad debt, don't just rest. Build.

- Work on opening new platforms of income or resource

generation. More income gives you leverage.

- Align your spending with your values. Buy what matters. Everything else is noise.
- Protect your peace: Avoid returning to the same debt patterns. Upgrade your identity: You are someone who lives above debt, not under it.

Debt isn't just financial. It's spiritual and emotional too, because it robs you of confidence, choice, and power. But when you demolish it—you reclaim yourself. You get time. Mental space. Energy. And that returns to you in every quadrant of prosperity: Wellness, Resources, Harmony, Significance.

Set a realistic time frame to achieve all this. That could be 120 days, it could be two years, depending on how much you owe and what your earning capacity is. Don't flirt with shortcuts— they cost more in faith, freedom, and ROI later.

Debt That Builds You…

Remember that not all debt is created equal.
Some debt is toxic, like financial crystal meth. It gives you a temporary high (the trendy watch or Vegas weekend), followed by a brutal comedown of regret, interest payments, and energy leaks.

But other debt? Used intentionally, it's leverage. And leverage, as you now know, is a superpower of wealth building. It's what you do to make sure you wake up every morning wealthier than you were when you went to sleep the night before.

If you borrow $400 to buy concert tickets, you're just another ignorant consumer trapped in the Matrix. (Getting played by the financial system we discussed in Chapter Eight.)

But if you borrow $700,000 to buy an income-producing property that throws off monthly cash flow, appreciates in value, and lets you legally deduct depreciation on your taxes— you're a wealth-building machine. You just used debt to buy an asset instead of a *liability.*

Lemme break it down for you: Broke people spend money on things that make them poorer. Wealthy people spend money on things that make them richer. So if you're not sure about a particular purchase, ask yourself…

Will this debt make me poorer or richer?

Purchases that create cash flow, appreciate over time, or increase your capability to earn more are smart debt. If buying something just scratches an emotional itch or gives you a dopamine hit, it's foolish debt.

This is how you flip the script from being owned by debt to owning wealth with it.

- Getting out of bad debt is phase one.
- Using strategic debt as a wealth lever is phase two.
- Becoming the kind of person who never needs to impress anyone with what they bought is phase three.

Debt can either drag down your life or supercharge your financial freedom. Choose mindfully—because once you master money, a new kind of challenge appears. Not the struggle to make it. But the chaos that comes when everyone around you suddenly wants a piece of it…

Chapter 10:

Homes for Unwed Llama Mamas & Other Brilliant Investments

Once you have money—Money with a capital M—some fascinating things begin to happen...

Your popularity begins to soar. Every week, your mailbox will be stuffed with invitations to birthday parties, baby showers, bar mitzvahs, Sweet 16 celebrations, weddings, and graduations. These will arrive from long-time, treasured acquaintances like the guy who installed your cable service and the bag boy at the supermarket. Distant cousins will hit you up to invest in their "can't miss" new venture selling Bus Bench Advertising in Beirut. Other friends and relatives will appeal for your support to finance their new charity providing homes for unwed llama mamas. You'll be receiving GoFundMe links to an endless stream of campaigns to save humanity by helping to finance treehouses, mancave remodeling projects, and boob jobs.

You probably spend a lot of time each morning swishing the mouthwash, fixing your hair, and selecting some nice clothes to present yourself to the world. But alas, to many people, this effort will be wasted because to them you will still look like an ATM.

Once you reach real prosperity, the question isn't can you make money. It becomes can you keep your sanity while everyone else tries to spend it for you. Let's look at how you can best navigate through this new dynamic…

First, recognize that some people are professional victims. Being unhappy makes them happy, because it allows them to play the victim card and receive certain types of emotional payoffs. For many, this becomes their identity, and they draw their sense of esteem from this. They're continually asking for money from you because they are continually manifesting situations where they are seemingly the innocent victim. (I know this because I used to be one. In my case, I was such an emotional cripple and hated myself so much, I couldn't accept love. In its place I substituted the attention and sympathy I received by always having drama and trauma in my life.)

At first, helping them out seems like the natural and prosperous way to respond. Unfortunately, this just reinforces the feedback loop. They create a calamity, you respond with attention, empathy, sympathy, caring, and, of course, money—and then they start the process all over again.

When you have people like this in your life, you can lovingly suggest self-development resources like podcasts, blogs, or this book. But know that none of them will have an impact until the victim grows tired of being a victim. You'll run out of money before they run out of tragedies.

People in this situation honestly believe they are innocent victims and have nothing to do with the ongoing drama they attract—and they simply can't understand your unwillingness to help them again and again and again and again. After all, you appear to have more than you "need," so why won't you share your wealth with them? As a result, you might find yourself being categorized as uncaring, selfish, or greedy.

In situations like this, be willing to let this happen. Love them and let them grow. Fund the scenarios you're comfortable funding and gently but lovingly refuse the rest. Maybe they break out, maybe they don't, but this has nothing to do with you or their perception of you. You can almost always find a better charity with a more compelling case to use your money wisely than whatever the individual victim manipulators are attempting to extort from you.

You might attract other perpetual victims who are also master manipulators. They have no shame and will employ any method of guilt, gaslighting, or even deceit to try to manipulate you into bailing them out of all the poor decisions they make in life.

They're constantly coming to you with emergencies like getting evicted, owing gambling debts, and having their wages garnished because they didn't pay the child support. And if you aren't willing to bail them out, they start running rackets on you…

They might say that you have so much wealth that the help they're asking for is meaningless to you. (Terrible premise.)

Or they say things like "If you were a good Christian (Buddhist, Jew, etc.), you would do this for me." Or they will suggest that *you* will be the person responsible for the bad consequences they will suffer because of their actions. Or they might propose that these are loans which they will pay back, even if there have been 813 previous loans defaulted on.

We all mess up occasionally, and if you have the resources to provide a "get out of jail free" card to rescue someone every now and then, by all means, do it. Sometimes an act of kindness like this makes a huge impact on someone's life and can be a catalyst for turning things around. And it's just nice to help others when you can.

But when someone keeps coming back to the well, using manipulation techniques, it's time to draw the line.
When I reach the breaking point, I'll say something like "I am going to give you this money, but you cannot ever pay me back. It's your final grant from the Randy Gage Foundation. Hopefully, you will find a way to pay it forward sometime in the future. But I must advise you that this is the last time I am willing to do this. If you should ever ask me for financial help again, I will end the conversation immediately." And I do.

They may try two or three more times, but eventually they stop asking, which usually means the relationship is done. Be okay with that. (Or else we need to work on *your* self-esteem.)

Then there is the final group—perhaps family members or other loved ones. You might care deeply for someone and recognize that they simply do not have the mental faculties or social skills to keep up in today's world. Some people just don't possess the self-awareness, resilience, or coping mechanisms required in difficult situations. Most importantly, these are not people who feel entitled, and they don't try to guilt or manipulate you. They're metaphorically adrift at sea, desperately hoping someone will come along and rescue them.

Situations like this allow you to practice the circulation law of prosperity. Give as you feel moved to, without expecting recognition or repayment. Just know that this makes the world—and your soul—richer.

Also know that prosperity always finds its way back. But it rarely returns quietly. It shows up louder, shinier, and faster. Which brings us to the next lesson…

What happens when your mindset still drives a Toyota…but your garage now holds a Bugatti.

Chapter 11:

You Bought the Bugatti—But You're Still Thinking Like a Toyota Owner

The other thing you're going to discover once you get Money—with a capital M—is that you now have many nice things, and many of the people in your world don't know how to treat them. (And neither do you.) This is why the cliché, *This is why we can't have nice things,* is a cliché.

As your wealth and prosperity consciousness grows, you'll be shopping in different places, having different experiences, and finding yourself in a completely new environment. This usually means you must rethink some of the people you do business with.

The car wash you used to take your Toyota to is not the one to use for your Bugatti. Unless you love having swirling scratches in your paint job.

The dry cleaner you used for your clothes from Target is not the one to take your new Brioni suits to. Unless you love having suits with smashed buttons, disfigured collars, and crumpled shoulders.

The housekeeper who dusts your Dogs Playing Poker print is not the same one you want dusting the new painting you just paid $650,000 for. Unless you love…well, let's just not go there.

The people who maintain your new treasures aren't the only ones who require adjustment...

Wealth and consciousness are inextricably linked. As you evolve, so will the world around you. Each new environment will demand fresh mindsets and behaviors. Once I had some money, I treated myself with Bally loafers, dope suits, and exotic supercars—much of which I destroyed quickly, because my consciousness hadn't evolved enough to know how to care for such items. You can skip that step in your journey if you will allow me to share some simple prosperity tips to help you ease into this new reality of a prosperous life more smoothly:

- Once you start buying top-quality shoes, you'll need to keep them in shape with shoe trees. And use a shoehorn when you put them on.

- The Bentley or Rolls-Royce dealership can recommend a great car detailer to keep your new investment in top shape.

- Most salaried employees at a bank or brokerage will have no idea how to give practical financial advice to an entrepreneur.

- Don't ask for wellness advice from out-of-shape people who drink, drug, or smoke. Even if (especially if) they're wearing a white lab coat and a stethoscope.

- The clerks at high-end clothing stores can also give you advice on which dry cleaner in your town knows how to take care of designer clothes.

- Wealth is dramatically easier to develop (and expand) as an entrepreneur than as an employee.

- Your new, tailored suits should always be stored on a wooden hanger, curved to protect the collar and shape.

- A banker or broker who earns $150k a year is not likely to be qualified to give advice for managing a portfolio of $10 million or more.

Reaching your next big breakthrough…

Okay, you've built a prosperous life; you've manifested Money with a capital M. Were Jim Rohn still alive today, he would remind you, "Once you get a million dollars, you better learn how to become a millionaire."

Because the real challenge isn't managing your money, maintaining optimal health, and developing loving, empowering relationships. It's creating the consciousness that produces those realities.

If you speak with my coaching and consulting clients, most of them credit me for helping them grow and scale rapidly because of the critical thinking strategies and marketing know-how I helped them integrate into their business. Elements like creating compelling copywriting, recognizing untapped markets, using social media effectively, applying ecommerce tactics, employing AI for better productivity, and similar items.

But I'd wager that in more than 75 percent of the cases, it was the mental mindset work we did before the tactics that produced the greatest breakthroughs...

The moment you picked up this book, you were vibrating at a certain consciousness. Most people begin in the doubt and fear zones, and once you teach them skills they can advance with, their confidence grows, and they start accelerating their progress. Sometimes they backslide or fall prey to imposter syndrome, because their old, negative mind viruses resurface. They need another boost of positive juice.

Not simply rah-rah motivation but specific help recognizing limiting beliefs they hold, blowing them up, and replacing them with empowering beliefs that serve the new version of who they have become.

Finally, they enter the place they really want to inhabit, the Continuous Improvement Zone. Each small victory along the way is increasing their belief, confidence, and self-esteem. Each success helps rewire their expectations at a higher level. Instead of expecting to lose, they expect to win. (See illustration.)

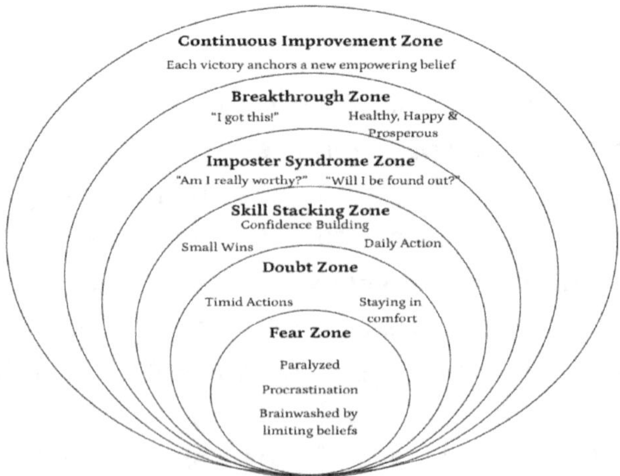

This goal of continuous growth is the ideal within my Breakthrough U program. This is a program I'm immensely proud of because it's the only one of its kind in the world. It's a combination growth accelerator, mastermind group, and coaching program. To get the best results, it's divided into three levels:

Apprentice Level: For people who are stuck, self-sabotaging, or even moving backwards. They're not aware of the limiting beliefs they have that are holding them back. The work here is exclusively on creating the right mindset for success and prosperity.

Alchemy Level: For those who are out there making moves but need to take the jump from six figures to seven.

Anarchist Level: For the one percent of the one percent. The place for rebels, misfits, and disrupters. They're over-achievers who are operating at a high level of success but desire to accelerate and scale.

It's a great thought exercise for you if you do some critical thinking about what level you are at in your own prosperity journey. You might think the people at the Anarchist Level have everything figured out, but you'd be wrong. They join sometimes because I'm the only person who will challenge their thinking. Or because they may have received the greatest awards in their field or are earning tens of millions of dollars—but their marriage is in ruins, their kids don't speak to them, or they're one hot fudge sundae away from a diabetic coma. Sometimes they're workaholics and need to learn how to have a real vacation, take days off, and have "no device" time. Often, it's to help them develop their charitable and contribution efforts.

I give the entrepreneurs in the program the same premise I'm offering you here: You are meant to be healthier, happier, and more prosperous.

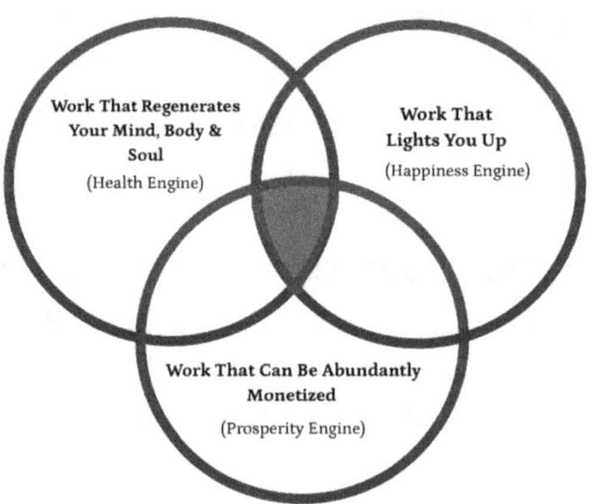

Sweet Spot of an Ideal Biz

Creating this type of business with a prosperous lifestyle means you must be in a mindset of expansion. Because the moment you stop expanding your awareness, your prosperity starts shrinking. And that brings us to what might be the most important dynamic in your journey…

The size of the window you see the world through.

An abundant life can occur only when you are continually growing, when your future is always greater than your past in some way. We must appreciate our past experiences, using them as catalysts for wisdom and growth. Likewise, we must live and celebrate the now. But that now becomes stagnant if there isn't a vision to do, have, and become more. In whatever way(s) matter most to you at this point in your life.

If you don't nurture your future vision—and expand the window through which you see the world—your consciousness atrophies and your fortune becomes your prison. So, let's break open that cell door in the next chapter.

Because when you finally step through, you'll discover something astonishing: thinking bigger isn't just a mindset… it's a multiplier.

Chapter 12:

Magnitude of Scale: Why Thinking Bigger Pays Better

'm currently conducting a comprehensive, groundbreaking, rigorous, cross-sectional, peer-reviewed, gold-standard, double-blind, placebo-controlled, first-of-its-kind, breakthrough, scientific research study. The purpose of the study is to test the following hypothesis:

In today's environment, it is easier to become a billionaire than a millionaire.

This premise may not be as cheeky as it sounds. As I told you earlier, it's surprisingly easier to earn a large amount of money quickly than it is to earn a small amount of money over a longer period. This is due in large part to a dynamic I call the "Magnitude of Scale Effect." Put simply…

The more bold, audacious, and breathtaking an endeavor is—the greater the likelihood it will attract the people and

resources necessary to bring it into existence.

Think about this: Airbnb went from two guys renting air mattresses to a $100 billion IPO faster than millions of entrepreneurs ever manage to reach six figures.

Why is it easier to sell a Lamborghini Veneno than a Ford Escape? The person who buys a Ford likely must plan far ahead, budget tightly, weigh sacrifices, and hopefully get approved for credit to drive home their new wheels. The person who buys a Lambo understands the concept of value-for-value exchange, has no creditworthiness issues, and brings in enough discretionary income to make the purchase an easy decision. Even an impulse one.

If you want to join me on my crusade to make the world more prosperous, it begins by increasing the level of your own prosperity. And the most important part of that process is expanding the window through which you see the world.

I use shoes as the analogy for how this process worked with me. Initially my dream was to be able to afford a pair of luxurious Bally loafers, which cost around $200 back then. Younger readers may be shocked to discover we didn't always live in a world where sneaker drops were a thing! My siblings and I had two pairs of shoes: dress shoes (cheap leather or, more often, plastic) which we wore to school, to church, on holidays, etc., and tennis shoes for gym and after school.

By the time I grew up and had entered the business world, having three or four pairs of shoes meant you were extremely rich. In fact, I knew a few guys who had black shoes for dark suits and brown shoes they could wear with a green or tan suit. I even saw Elvis on television once wearing blue suede shoes!

Next thing you know, I'm a twenty-something hard-charger who wants to be a business tycoon like Bobby Ewing on Dallas and Blake Carrington on Dynasty, and I heard about the aforementioned Bally loafers. (Which were voted by the readers of Robb Report magazine as the most comfortable shoes in the world.) Since $200 was what I paid to buy my used car from the post office government auction, you can imagine what a daunting, almost impossible goal this was for me.

But manifest those suckers I did.

Had my mother learned at that time that I spent $200 on a pair of shoes, she would have slapped me into next week. But the spell was broken…

I learned there was another world reality out there, and that it was possible for a kid from Allied Drive in Madison, Wisconsin, to own nice things. Once I started rocking those Ballys—the window I saw the world through started expanding.

Next thing you know, I'm sporting Prada and Hugo Boss sneakers costing $500 a pair. I learned that when your dream is big enough, you can bend the Universe to your will. Of course, I was spending money like a drunken sailor (if sailors wore Prada sneakers), trying to convince myself that I'd never go back to having just two pairs of shoes.

Within a few years, I'm shelling out a thousand dollars a pair for Donna Karan combat boots and Testoni Oxfords. One weekend after regaling my prosperity seminar audience with tales of my shoe collection, one of the attendees alerts me to Lobb's of London—bespoke shoemaker to the Royal Family. They create wooden molds of your feet, handcrafting each shoe: one person cuts the leather, another stitches by hand, another sets the rivets, etc.

Within a few weeks, I've booked flights BA001 & BA002 (aka the British Airways NY-London run on the Concorde) for a weekend of shoe shopping, getting my feet personally measured by John Lobb, the third generation of the clan. Not only did I break the sound barrier but also the $10,000-per-pair-of-shoes barrier. (And as a bonus became a time traveler, arriving back in Gotham City ninety minutes before I left London.)

Another fun fact: When I was renewing my insurance one year and told my agent that I had $150,000 worth of shoes to insure, she literally started shrieking.

I could amuse you with similar stories about the expanding consciousness process with my purchases of watches, artwork, automobiles, and other various bling-bling. (In fact, I once bought three different colors of the same Viper SRT so when I went out for dinner, my car could match my shoes.)

But at some point, you'd probably find the stories less inspiring and more irritating. (If you haven't already.) If you find yourself flinching at these stories of ostentatious wealth, here's a few things to think about…

First, I didn't start by flying Concorde. I was the guy in the middle seat in Row 35 across from the lav. And I wasn't like the grifter influencers you see today, debt peacocking or renting exotic cars by the day for their vapid social media posts. (Pretending to be a Lambo baller when they're really Lambroke.) I paid cash for everything and used those purchases to fuel bigger dreams, create a larger window through which to see the world, and, as a result, was able to solve enough problems and create enough value that the Universe kept rewarding me with more and greater prosperity.

No doubt, I was an arrogant, insecure, nouveau riche kid spending money foolishly. But looking back, I wouldn't change a thing. I've since learned how to become a good steward of money and grown comfortable in my own skin. In fact, my greatest prosperity superpower these days is not needing to signal my virtue or wealth to anyone. But that ferocious spending was a phase I needed to go through to completely eviscerate the poverty consciousness I was programmed with. And as Bobby Axelrod says, "What's the point of having fuck-you money if you don't say 'fuck you' to the people who deserve it?"

But second, you may want to consider what makes you recoil at these stories. How much of your reaction is kneejerk programming and how much came from mindful reflection? What are your core foundational beliefs about money, wealthy people, and luxurious lifestyles?

Your version of this chapter may not be shoes—it might begin by sending your first invoice with confidence, saying no to a lowball offer, or asserting boundaries to someone trying to kill your dream. The point here isn't monetary costs but the principle of prosperity consciousness.

If you're like me, you might have grown up thinking that $50,000 a year is a large income. Once you reach that, you'd probably decide that $100,000 or $200,000 is a lot. But if the window you see the world through is continually expanding, at some point you might be spending more for an automobile than you used to spend for a house.

And that's when it hits you: the most seductive, dangerous, prosperity-killing question of them all.

Four little words that sound reasonable…but will wreck your wealth if you believe them.

Chapter 13:

The Most Dangerous Question in Prosperity...

How much is enough?

That question is possibly one of the most lack-centered statements ever uttered. Because it's almost never asked by someone doing a real philosophical analysis, wondering about the cause-and-effect relationship that money and material things might have on our happiness.

Usually, the question is used to suggest the person being asked the question is greedy, selfish, and materialistic. (It feeds the programming that many people have that it is somehow noble or spiritual to be poor.) That question is usually followed by comments about how many shirts you can wear in one day, how a car only takes you from point A to point B, and other lack-centered beliefs.

You don't have to replicate my crazed material acquisition

display detailed in the last chapter. Although I won't begrudge you if you do. In fact, I'll celebrate your overindulgence with you. As long as your actions ultimately take you to the important payoff: Recognizing any limiting beliefs about money, material things, health, and relationships that no longer serve you—then blowing them up—and replacing them with empowering beliefs of prosperity consciousness. Understanding that all true forms of prosperity are infinite.

Here's something else that's important to understand…

You don't manifest any form of true prosperity—including money—by taking it from someone else.

Because all forms of prosperity are infinite, it is not required for others to have less for you to manifest more. When you manifest any form of prosperity on the physical plane, you are creating more abundance, which produces yet more expanding energy. It is a self-sustaining cycle of wealth. Prosperity manifestation is stunted only when it is harbored and hoarded. When you circulate prosperity, it continues to generate more positive, prosperous energy.

Let's use an analogy here to illustrate when this "how much is enough" question may be unwarranted and lead you away from true prosperity...

Would you ask how much love was enough? Or kindness? What about health? Imagine making the following statement, "Look at that Jeannie. She is so healthy it makes me angry. Other people have injuries, cancer, and heart attacks—and she's hoarding all the good health for herself."

That would be ludicrous because health is not a regulated resource. There is not a limited supply requiring one person to have poor health for another to experience wellness.

All elements that comprise true prosperity are renewable resources that infinitely replenish themselves to replace the portion depleted by use. An example is renewable energy: Solar, geothermal, and wind energy all can restock themselves. I postulate that the same concept is true for the elements of prosperous living…

These prosperity elements are continuously replenished by the Universe because they are infinite. Take love, compassion, or hugs for example. They're certainly infinite. You can give away ten hugs and that doesn't deplete the inventory, leaving fewer hugs to go around. I would argue that giving away ten hugs increases the inventory, because the more you give away, the more you receive. This is true for joy, love, harmony, compassion, forgiveness, empathy, understanding, and all the other elements of true prosperity.

When I present this concept in my books and seminars, most people readily accept this. But for some reason, they believe that one vital element of prosperity—money—is somehow different. Most people think that money is a finite resource—one that requires taking from one person to provide to another.

But that's a bad premise...

There is nothing that makes currencies like the U.S. dollar, British pound, or Mexican peso finite. These are fiat currencies, and as such are not backed by anything more than a government's promise to pay. They have value only when we go along with the dubious proposition that governments keep their promises.

Government currencies have no intrinsic value of their own; they're legislatively enabled pyramid schemes. When governments require more money, they just print more. Therefore, money is simply a meme we've created to try and mentally understand the process of trading value. Once you remove the government machinations, what determines money's worth is the value exchanged for it. There is no finite value for money. As long as you are willing to provide new methods of value, there will be an infinite supply of money available to you.

On the surface, Bitcoin might appear to be a finite resource to you, as there is only a guaranteed amount to be mined and it is regulated on a blockchain. But this definition misses out on the way we use money. Like other currencies, Bitcoin has no static fixed value. The value is determined in the commerce of free trade. So, while there may be a finite number of Bitcoin, there is no ceiling on the value for each.

The "real" element of prosperity is the value you create that can be exchanged. There are two ways you can endlessly manifest prosperity:
- Solving problems
- Adding value

When you solve problems or add value, people will lovingly, joyfully, and gratefully crawl naked over broken glass to throw money at you.

Even better, there are no limits on the number of problems

you can solve or value you can add. If you have jury duty and someone can walk your dog while you're trapped in the courthouse, you'll gladly pay them $35 to solve the problem of your puppy pooping on your new rug. If you have an abscessed tooth, you will joyfully pay a dentist $1,000 to make your pain go away. And if a hurricane comes by and blows your roof off, you'll happily give someone $25,000 to slap on a new one as soon as you can find them. What this means for prosperity is:

The bigger the problems you can solve, the more money people will be willing to trade to you.

There is also no limit to the amount of value you can add... Remember the Magnitude of Scale. If you can show your cousin how to whack a golf ball farther, she might buy you lunch. If you can show someone who wants to make the college golf team how to hit farther, she might hire you as a swing coach for $75 a lesson. If you can show Sung Hyun Park how to drive farther, she might pay you $300,000 a year. Simple math: The higher the degree of value you can provide, the more money people will be willing to trade to you.

Please don't think only in terms of material things. Just because you don't have a luxury home or an exotic supercar to sell, your ability to manifest prosperity is not curbed. If you can teach someone how to do something—speak your language, reconcile with a family member, regain their health, cook ethnic food, raise their bowling score, or, God forbid, post an Instagram reel—there is an endless stream of people who would love to trade their money with you.

The value you provide to the Universe determines the amount of prosperity you can receive back. And there are no limitations on this because the same principle applies to your talents and gifts. When you share them, they expand and become stronger.

Money follows value. Create more value. Attract more money. Ain't it great!

This value that you circulate expands its own energy, which creates ripple effects of prosperity, which ultimately find their way back to you. It is a self-replicating cycle that goes on forever.

This is why a prosperous person never seeks to acquire money just for the sake of acquiring it. Money is simply the medium of exchange for the things you really want. (A safe home, good-quality health care, free time to enjoy with loved ones, etc.) Money—just like health, relationships, love, empathy, and other manifestations of true prosperity—truly is an infinite resource.

If wealth was finite, humankind could have never progressed from our survival existence of hunting and gathering. The more value you create for the world, the more prosperous you will become. It is a law of the Universe.

Your goal is not to acquire more money. Your real goal is to solve enough problems and provide enough value to attract as much money as you need to trade for the prosperous life you desire to live. And your ability to do that isn't finite but infinite.

Remember the teachings of Wallace D. Wattles that we explored at the beginning of the book? To make the world more prosperous, you must become more prosperous. This dynamic can play out in you only if you are mindfully and systematically expanding the window you view the world through. Seeking to do, have, and become more, seeking to reach the highest possible version of yourself. It serves no one—absolutely no one—for you to keep playing small.

Please. Stop looking for reasons to limit your thinking, hold back your actions, and dial down your goals. Every dream in your mind is the Universe tapping on the door, inviting you to become a higher version of yourself. The amount of prosperity and abundance you manifest is a direct result of the value you create and the problems you solve. To have a better world...

We need you to be rich. In all senses of the word. Because the world doesn't get better when good people play small.

Because the world doesn't need more broke dreamers—it needs awake creators. And when you finally stop apologizing for your prosperity...

You unleash it to prosper the world.

Chapter 14:

From Success to Significance: Prosperity's Final Test

Prosperity has one final test for you: Can you give without keeping score? Because at some point you stop asking, How much can I earn? and start pondering, How much can I contribute?

This is when your prosperity either imprisons you or liberates you. Your life morphs from being a business plan to a mission. The intoxicating adventure of becoming the highest possible version of yourself.

Don't get me wrong: The trips, cars, accolades, money, and recognition are all great. But the best reward is who you become.

And that really is the thesis for this book. There is an evolution we must go through to manifest the abundance that is our birthright. Think of it as a spiritual hero's journey for the modern wealth creator.

One caveat to note…

In most cases, this journey of the hero continually facing obstacle after obstacle is frequently self-created, because we fall prey to bad programming along the way.

A newborn baby or a toddler are perfect demonstrations of prosperity consciousness. If we all kept that innocence and developed from there, our journey to manifesting a prosperous joyful life would be elegant and clearcut. Unfortunately, from birth, we're almost immediately assaulted with programming of lack and limitation.

How many times do you think you were told, "Stop," "Don't touch that," and "No" in your first three or four years? As we discussed earlier, the current culture attacks us with a multitude of factors such as fear, self-doubt, worthiness issues, and entitlement thinking to contaminate our thought processes from a very early age. Recent developments like the pandemic, isolation, and social media have exacerbated the process. As a result, for most of us, our prosperity journey began in the same neighborhood:

Victimhood.

You don't choose to move into that hood consciously. You just wake up one day realizing you've been paying rent in resentment, blame, and excuses. It's the emotional ghetto where people worship limitation and confuse suffering with virtue.

I can conduct an all-day seminar on prosperity and have a

thousand people nodding along in sage agreement with everything I'm teaching about victimhood. The second it wraps up, 982 of them will then get in line to explain to me why, in their unique case, they are simply a random, innocent bystander victim to whom these principles don't apply.

Scroll through a social media platform today and it seems like a moral competition to prove you are the most wronged gender, race, religion, political party, occupation, or all the above. If you were an alien from another planet and happened to drop by Earth to study the species known as human, you'd probably assume most people were competing in a Victimhood Olympics.

Victimhood is emotional poverty. It's the belief that life happens to you instead of through you. That you're a pawn on someone else's chessboard.

People in this state are easily recognized by the clues they give up. They're not happy unless they're miserable. They are even more miserable if you're not miserable for them. They wear being victimized almost as a badge of honor. It's the only lens through which they see the world.

Because they have low self-esteem, they unknowingly use their negative circumstances to justify their worthiness. Eventually they end up manifesting and attracting worse treatment—to justify this perverted vision they have of themselves.

You can't create prosperity from that vibration because victimhood kills your agency. Prosperity requires power—and power flows only through self-responsibility. The good news is that the moment you recognize victimhood as a choice, you've already outgrown it.

When you stop asking, Why is this happening to me? and start asking, What am I doing to attract or contribute to this?—the locks on your cell door click open.

The next step is reframing (perhaps de-guilting) how you see money and success...

Most of us were conditioned to feel guilty for wanting more—as if ambition were a moral flaw instead of a divine impulse. But money is simply energy. It magnifies who you already are and flows toward clarity, purpose, and value.

True prosperity begins the moment you stop apologizing for wanting more and start believing you are worthy of receiving it. Because worthiness isn't arrogance—it's alignment.

Not everyone starts in victimhood, nor does everyone have to reframe their core foundational beliefs. But most people do have to work through some issues to stop the self-sabotage they've been unwittingly doing to themselves. Going through this process and removing any blocks are necessary for you to take that next jump from success to significance.

When prosperity matures, it turns into purpose. You stop chasing more and start creating meaning. You realize your wealth was never meant to be a monument—it was meant to be a movement.

Significance is success multiplied by service. It's when your prosperity stops being about you—and starts being about what moves through you.

This is why rich people give away so much. It's not just because they have it to give. It's because they have become people who give. Here's what this hierarchy looks like for many people:

The Prosperity Hierarchy

SIGNIFICANCE (Purpose, Contribution, Legacy)
MAGNITUDE Of SCALE EFFECT (Bold Thinking, Big Vision)
MONEY MASTERY (Learning the Money Game, Smart Debt)
CONSCIOUSNESS ALIGNMENT (Worthiness, Identity, Divine Discontent)
DEFINING PROSPERITY (The 4 Quadrants)
BREAKING FREE (Eviscerating Limit Beliefs & Programming)
AWARENESS (Trading Victimhood for Agency)

Prosperity has never been about accumulating things. Prosperity is about becoming someone—the kind of person through whom the Universe can safely channel infinite abundance. When you transcend victimhood, detox guilt, and embody worthiness—manifesting money becomes effortless, and meaning becomes inevitable. Because in the end, true prosperity isn't what you have, it's what you're here to give. Which brings us back to...

You.

There may be no endeavor more noble for you to pursue than becoming healthy, happy, and prosperous yourself. Because if your own needs aren't being met, you're not much good to the rest of us. We need you to live rich.

You don't serve the world by being unhappy, unhealthy, or poor. A diminished you creates a diminished world. And there are systems that profit from your pain. Not necessarily because they're evil in concept, but because they're designed for dependency.

- You're no good to big pharma and the hospital complex if you're dead. But you're very lucrative to them if you're sick.

- You're no good to the political parties and social media platforms if you're happy. But you're very lucrative to them if you're angry and afraid.

- You're no good to the credit card companies and financial institutions if you're bankrupt. But you're very lucrative to them if you're financially illiterate and perpetually struggling with debt.

It begins with you…

You don't make the world more prosperous by controlling others or using your will to influence anyone or anything except yourself. (Even if you believe that control is for their own good. Especially if you believe it's for their own good.) For worldwide prosperity to unfold, it does not require you to force or manipulate another. Nor does global prosperity require you to submit any list of desires (demands) of any deity.

Be mindful of your own thinking, practice your own discipline, and follow the principles we've discussed. Visualize your own highest good and allow your own subconscious mind to direct your actions to manifest it. When you become more prosperous, the world becomes more prosperous.

Should you encounter a starving person, give them food if you are able. But for most people in poverty, what they require more than a meal is inspiration. They need a role model to follow, someone to demonstrate that breaking the cycle of scarcity and ignorance is possible. And the only way to demonstrate that becoming prosperous is doable is by doing it yourself.

The best way we eradicate poverty from Earth is by teaching people the principles contained in this book. (Please join me in holding the vision that this book becomes one of the most frequent graduation gifts ever given. And not just college. For many, that's already way late. Kids need this information in high school and middle school. Even if I do drop the occasional 'F' bomb!)

Societies don't become prosperous on their own. Prosperous societies are made up of prosperous people. People like you and me. If we truly want to make the world an abundant place, it is our sacred responsibility to become the most prosperous possible versions of ourselves. Put in its simplest terms…

The best way to help the poor, the downtrodden, and the exploited—is to make sure you're not one of them.

You beat the bad actors when you have agency; when you bust out and create your own destiny; when you become healthy, happy, and prosperous.

When you rise, the frequency of the entire world rises with you. So let me say it...One. More. Time.

The world needs you to be healthy.
The world needs you to be happy.
The world needs you to be rich.

You up for that?

<u>Mad Love To….</u>

They say a committee is where brilliant ideas go to be slowly strangled to death. And they're usually right. Committees dilute genius, sand down the edges, and compromise the very spark that makes bold thinking bold.

But a mastermind—that's a different force entirely...

A true mastermind doesn't dilute brilliance—it amplifies it. It creates a vortex where great ideas collide, fornicate, and grow into something exponentially more powerful than any one person could produce alone. This book was born in that vortex. It is the product of a remarkable mind-meld of people who challenged, provoked, and inspired me—and refused to let me play small. Readers of the early drafts of the manuscript who provided insightful ideas included **Alan Weiss, Jaime Lokier, Erick Gamio, Wes Linden, Bill Bachrach, and Bob Burg.**

Working more than 200 cover concepts down to the one you're holding was a journey in its own right. Special thanks to the people above along with **Kamal Ravikant, Jose Lopez, Dana Collins, Christian Riander, Fabio Correia, JJ Birden, Anna Liotta, Payam Moghim** and, in a publishing first, my sister **Liese.**

At this point in my journey, I couldn't imagine penning a book without the legendary editing services of **Vicki McCown,** who keeps me out of the ditches. She reduces the profanity and increases the value.

And **Samuel Hasbun**, for helping coordinate all those interactions, providing charts, and other helpful assistance. Everyone named, and many who were not, contributed in a generous way to help craft a book that would provide more value to you. Please raise a glass, make a toast, and appreciate them as I do.

Other "Must Read" Books by Randy…

Other Resources from Randy:

Website and Success Blog:
https://randygage.com/

Randy's Power Prosperity Podcast:
https://randygage.com/podcast

Breakthrough U Growth Accelerator:
https://randygage.com/breakthroughu/